SIREN RESOURCES
Presents

How to Write a Story

J.J. Barnes

For Jane Elliott and Steph Warren

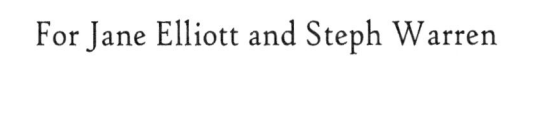

Contents

	Foreword	009
I	My First Piece of Writing Advice	011
II	The "Protagonist/Antagonist Dynamic"	014
III	"Conflict" in a Story?	017
IV	The "Inciting Incident"	021
V	The "Midpoint"	024
VI	The "Three-Act Structure"	027
VII	How to Write Foreshadowing	030
VIII	The Balance Between Protagonist and Antagonist	035
IX	Multiple Protagonists	039
X	Multiple Antagonists	044
XI	Pacing Your Story	048
XII	Avoid Writing a Passive Protagonist	052
XIII	Making Your Characters Distinct	055
XIV	Writing Flawed Characters	059
XV	Motivating Your Villains	063
XVI	Show Don't Tell	066
XVII	World Building	070
XVIII	How to Write Flashbacks	076
XIX	"Narrative Triplets"	080
XX	Deaths of Main Characters	084
XXI	Character Backstory	087
XXII	Writing Natural Dialogue	091
XXIII	The Lie Your Protagonist Believes	094
XXIV	From the Mundane to the Magical	097
XXV	Time-Locks	100
XXVI	The "Death of the Mentor"	103
XXVII	Coincidences	107
XXVIII	How to Write Suspense	112
XXIX	Making the Unbelievable Believable	116
XXX	Your Character's Arc	120
XXXI	Exploring the Point of View Character Concept	126
XXXII	Making Characters' Motivations Understandable	130
XXXIII	How to Make Your Audience Cry	134
XXXIV	Launching a Series with a Cliffhanger	138
XXXV	Writing Enemies to Friends	142
XXXVI	Death and Resurrection	145
XXXVII	How to Write Plot Twists	150
XXXVIII	Writing Info Dumps	154
XXXIX	Perfecting Your Prose to Dialogue Ratio	160
XL	How to Write Chapter One	165
XLI	How to Track Your Continuity	172
XLII	Editing	176
XLIII	Writer's Block	182

Foreword

I met J.J. Barnes online in November 2014. Our first conversation was about a book she was writing. Our second was about a book *I* was writing. Neither of us had been published or self-published at that time, because we didn't really know how a good story was put together then.

What followed as we continued to date, and began to fall in love, was a growing shared obsession with the craft of storytelling.

Books, movies, TV shows, comics—all of these were on the table for absolute deconstruction. We would dismantle our favourite stories and then put them back together again.

We started recording podcasts, where we'd sit and deep-dive on our favourite stories—and we finished and published those books which had been the subject of our very first chats.

She released *Lilly Prospero and the Magic Rabbit*, and I released *Emily the Master Enchantress*; both the firsts in a pair of series.

Since then we've published dozens of novels, novellas and short stories; had a TV pilot produced; and made an indie movie with our talented friends.

And if you're reading this there's a good chance you've seen J.J. (and possibly me) on YouTube. It was on YouTube that we started really giving away the lessons we'd learned, many of which have been collected here under the apt title: *How to Write a Story*.

Because that's what this is ...

A collection of incredibly practical lessons in the craft we've obsessed over together for more than half a decade.

You'll read the word "Protagonist" a lot. You'll read the word "goal" a lot. You'll read the phrase "what your Protagonist wants" a lot, because character, motivation and conflict genuinely are the building blocks of all your favourite tales.

J.J. will arm you with wisdom that has been shared for millennia, as far back as Aristotle's Poetics; she'll arm you with wisdom which has developed over the last hundred years through the culture of cinema; and she'll arm you with tricks and tips she and I cooked up here in our home while cooking dinner and sharing (a few too many) bottles of wine.

If you want to write a story and you just can't figure out how to pull it off, I promise you that by the time you're finished with this book you'll be so inspired and informed that it'll seem easier than ever before.

Enjoy, and all the best,

Jonathan McKinney

I
My First Piece of Writing Advice

When you're a writer, people will often tell you that they too want to write a book. They have ideas, maybe a character or a concept, but they're just not sure how to start it. And I always give them the same piece of advice:

1. Work out who your main character is
2. Work out what they want
3. Work out what's stopping them have it

Your story is your character in pursuit of something. So, you start with your character realising they want something, then through the story you send them after it, throwing challenges in their way. You end your story when they either get the thing they want or realise they can't have it.

Sometimes through the story they will realise that the thing they're in pursuit of isn't what they wanted after all. Their journey is taking them back to learning that what they wanted was there all along.

What Your Character Wants

The best example of communicating what your character wants can be seen in any Disney movie.

Disney movies will start with an "I Want Song". Simba sings that he can't wait to be king, his story follows him on his path to becoming King of the Pride Lands. Ariel sings about wanting to be part of the human world, and her story follows her on her path to becoming a human. Moana sings about her desire to go out onto the ocean, and her story follows her on her path to leading her people off on boats to explore the world. You know immediately what those characters want, and what story you're going to be following.

Jack Skellington in *The Nightmare Before Christmas* is a good example of a story following a character in pursuit of what they think they want, only to realise they were wrong. Jack feels dissatisfied with his life in Halloween Town and pursues the dream of being the Santa Claus but comes to realise his satisfaction can be found at home, but with Sally.

Sometimes your character will get what they want, sometimes they won't, but your story always follows them in pursuit of it.

Books and films for children communicate the "I want" in a simple and clear way. In *Nature-Girl Vs Worst Nightmare*, the book I wrote with my daughter, Nature-Girl expresses the desire to be a superhero without any of the adults in her life getting in the way or holding her back in the first few pages. You know immediately what the character wants, and what she will be setting out to do.

To write the equivalent into a book aimed at adults, tell your audience what the character wants but in a subtler way. It is still be the point of the story, it just gets woven into their frustrations and emotions more than being explicitly stated.

Focus Your Story on What Your Character Wants

When you're telling your story, keep the character's motivation and what they're in pursuit of in mind the whole way through. If you let yourself get distracted your story will start to wander and you can get lost, which makes the story feel aimless and can be quite boring for the reader.

Even if there are competing goals for your character, sub plots, and other events going on around them, your main character should always be actively working to achieve their goals.

II
The "Protagonist/Antagonist Dynamic"

The terms "protagonist" and "antagonist" appear commonly in all the writing advice. However, if you're unfamiliar with what they mean, this will be confusing. So, I'm going to explain what they are, what they do in your story, and how to write them well. I'm referencing the film *Terminator 2: Judgement Day*.

The Relationship Between Protagonist and Antagonist

Some people will use the term "protagonist" as interchangeable with main character or hero, but it's inaccurate. Protagonist literally means "the opponent of primary importance," descended from Greek. It's important to understand that a Protagonist cannot exist without an Antagonist. Without an Antagonist, there is no Protagonist.

The Antagonist can be human, but it isn't necessarily. The Antagonist can be a force of nature or fate for instance, but for the sake of this piece, I'll be writing about the Protagonist and the Antagonist when they both take the form of an active character within your story.

Your story is following your protagonist in pursuit of something they want, and your antagonist is the person that is trying to stop them getting it. That is the main conflict of your story.

Terminator 2

Terminator 2: Judgment Day is an excellent example to use when explaining the Protagonist and the Antagonist, because the Protagonist, Terminator, and the Antagonist, T-1000, are both in pursuit of the same thing. They both want John Connor, and they can't both have him.

They are locked in conflict. Terminator wants to protect him, T-1000 wants to kill him, they are both actively pursuing their goals. John Connor cannot both be killed and saved. One has to win; one has to lose.

Whilst almost perfectly matched in strength and ability, in *Terminator 2: Judgment Day*, the Antagonist is actually slightly superior to the Protagonist. In a straight fight, the T-1000 would in. This means the Protagonist has to go on a journey, a character arc, in order to achieve his goal over the Antagonist.

Clear Motivations

Terminator 2: Judgment Day is a really simple and clear story to study to properly understand the concept of the Protagonist and the Antagonist. Both characters are single minded in their motivations and story goals, and you immediately know who wants what and why.

When you're writing, you'll likely find you write both Protagonist and Antagonist having multiple goals, multiple motivations, around the one main goal, but the pure and clean conflict between Terminator and T-1000 is an excellent introduction.

One of the reasons *Terminator 2: Judgment Day* is such a popular and excellent story is because of the very clear lines of conflict between the Protagonist and Antagonist. Going into this film you know exactly what you're rooting for, exactly what you're invested in, and exactly what the story is.

Keep the Story Focused

More complicated layers of motivation do not necessarily make a story better. Having no distractions from the main storyline makes it easy to care about what happens.

If your story is too complicated and you're feeling like it's overwhelming and hard to follow, it's worth looking at the main conflict between your Protagonist and Antagonist and refocusing in on that. Simple and focused story telling is not a bad thing.

III
"Conflict" in a Story?

In most of these pieces of writing advice, I reference the conflict, because there is no story without conflict. I'll be explaining what conflict is, what it does for your story, and how to make sure you use it in your own work.

Your Character Wants Something They Don't Have

Conflict is, essentially, when your characters want something they don't have or can't have. For the sake of your story, what your characters want should be something attainable, but there's something in the way that they have to overcome in order to get it.

If your characters want something which they have no hope of getting, there's no story there because they've got nothing they can work for and do in order to satisfy that desire. Your story is watching them work for their goals, and either achieve them or not, whilst somebody or something works against them to stop them getting it.

Scenes Without Conflict

It's quite easy to go into a scene and forget to include conflict. When I first started writing, I would write characters having conversations, characters doing things, and they'd be going about their day to day life living. But there was no story. It was just following an existence. But following an existence without conflict isn't entertaining. It might be believable in a general way, because not every moment of real life is filled with conflict, but it doesn't make for an interesting story.

When you start telling your story, think about why you're telling your story *now* in this character's life. The reason you're jumping into their life now is because of their conflict. It's the thing they want right now that they have to try and work for. The story will have constant conflict because you're following them trying to get it. When they get it, the story is over because the conflict has been resolved.

Day to day life isn't conflict ridden like this, you'll have moments of conflict, but for the most part people are going about their day to day life without some quest or story they're being driven by at all times.

Finding Conflict in Ordinary Life

The only time you'll need to find permanent conflict in ordinary day to day life situations is if you're writing a soap opera. In soaps, ordinary day to day life of going to the supermarket, taking your children to school, walking the dog in the park, going to your job and working, all have to be laden with conflict or your soap will get boring and people won't bother.

But trying to find conflict in ordinary life in this way is why soaps are often dramatic to the point of being ridiculous and unbelievable, because there's only so much conflict that can naturally occur in that situation, without pushing circumstances to the extreme.

Finding Your Conflict

Regarding stories that are told via books and films, the audience is jumping into a character's life at that moment to witness a specific conflict. A specific story. The writer isn't trying to chronicle day to day life because that's not the point of the story. The story is following a character on something that *isn't* day to day life because they're trying to get something that changes their life.

A TV show that isn't a soap, but still follows day to day life, will be built around a specific concept. Perhaps it'll be a police show like *Blue Bloods*, or something supernatural like *Buffy the Vampire Slayer*. That concept requires something called a Conflict Generator.

If you take the TV series *Supernatural*, the conflict engine is that they are looking to solve supernatural mysteries and travelling around to help people. You don't watch Sam and Dean going to the bank or for lunch for no reason just because they're living their lives. You watch them as they are on their mini movie style conflict each week. In *Angel*, Doyle, and later Cordelia, receive visions of the people they need to help. In *Scrubs*, different patients come in with different heath needs. In *Firefly*, they have to keep getting different jobs that send them to different planets.

Behind the episodic conflict, you have the long form story conflict which is usually more soap opera style, which is the human relationships and the conflict between the characters that continues episode by episode as background to the episodic conflict.

Overall Conflict vs Scene-Level Conflict

When you write your story, work out what the conflict is overall, the thing your Protagonist is looking for and why they don't have it. It can be something supernatural like monsters attacking, or something mundane like somebody looking for a new job or relationship. But there's something your character wants, something they don't have, and something standing in the way of them getting it that they have to overcome. That is your story conflict.

Then, in each scene, look at the people in that scene, work out what they want in that moment and work out why they can't have it. Perhaps somebody wants to talk about one thing and somebody else wants to talk about something else, or there's disagreement over the thing they should do. It can be anything as long as the characters in that scene have an unsatisfied want. If everybody has what they want, and there's no conflict, there's no story.

IV
The "Inciting Incident"

I'm going to explain what the "Inciting Incident" is in your story, where to put it, what it's used for, and how to write it. I'll be referencing the film *The Matrix* as an example of a really well written inciting incident.

Triggering the Start of Your Story

The inciting incident is the event that triggers the start of your story. Prior to the inciting incident, your character was living their life, but not in active pursuit of their story goal. The inciting incident triggers the change. It sets them into active motion, from passive.

In *The Matrix*, it's when Trinity sends Neo the message to his computer telling him to follow the white rabbit.

Lock the Conflict

The inciting incident serves to lock the conflict between your protagonist and your antagonist. From this point you are following them both in pursuit of something and trying to stop the other from winning.

Because Neo is the Protagonist, the conflict that is launched by the inciting incident is the conflict between Neo and the Matrix itself. The Matrix is essentially a character in its own right.

The conflict lock between Neo and the Matrix is triggered by Neo being sent on the journey to discover the Matrix so he can do something to change it and expose it. The Matrix does not want anything to change and wants to carry on as it has been. They both want something, but they can't both have it. The Matrix can't both be exposed and continue to exist uninterrupted.

Pursuing a Goal

You want your Protagonist to be a person, or at least a robot, so the inciting incident causes them to make a choice to pursue a goal. By making an active choice to go after what they want, they are choosing to begin their story.

Until the inciting incident in *The Matrix*, Neo following the girl with the white rabbit tattoo, he is not involved in the story and is not pursuing his goal. He has no knowledge of the Matrix; he has no connection to anything that is happening. He has not been set against The Matrix. But the moment he goes to follow the white rabbit, he is on his path and we are following his story.

Where Does the Inciting Incident Go?

You can spend some time with your characters prior to the inciting incident. Show them existing in their lives and what may be missing, so when the inciting incident happens you understand why they make the choice to go after that goal. Use that time to let your audience connect with an understand why they become active now, why they are motivated to accomplish their goal.

However, you shouldn't spend too long prior to the inciting incident, because that's not your story and that's not why your audience has come to your work. Your inciting incident needs to go in the first act; in a book it should go in the first couple of chapters, in a film it should go in the first ten pages.

A lot of stories will spend time with the antagonist or with the villain of the story before going to the protagonist's inciting incident. For instance, in *The Matrix* you start with Trinity fighting agents and going out of the window. This allows the audience to see what is at stake for the Protagonist when their story is started.

In *Lilly Prospero and the Mermaid's Curse*, I started the story with the Antagonist; The Harvester. I show him dragging a mermaid from the ocean, preparing to harvest her body parts to sell on the magical black market. This immediately tells you what Lilly will be set against, so when her story is triggered, the audience understands why it matters.

V
The "Midpoint"

The "Midpoint" in your story comes when you've done all the set up in your story, and acts as a pivot to steer it towards the climax. You have got your Protagonist and your Antagonist locked in conflict, and they're both motivated towards achieving what they want to achieve, and now you need to start the process of crashing them together to see who wins.

I'll explain where in your timing that your midpoint comes, what it does for your story, and how to write an effective midpoint.

Where Does Your Midpoint Come?

The midpoint comes half-way through your second act, right in the middle of your story. Sometimes the midpoint is so game changing that writers will opt for a four-act structure as the midpoint breaks act two into two clear and distinct parts.

Whether you choose to write in three or four acts, your midpoint works to reframe your story and push your characters into their journey towards the end.

Examples of Effective Midpoints

This pivot can happen in a number of different ways. The film *Titanic* is an excellent example of how you can use your midpoint.

The start of the film is following Jack and Rose and their love story. They meet and fall in love, and then they are motivated to find a way to be together after the ship has docked in the USA.

At an hour and a half into the three-hour movie, they crash into an iceberg which changes the entire story. You are no longer watch Jack and Rose falling in love and wanting to find a way to be together, you are now watching them wanting to find a way to survive. It's very effective and offers immediate high stakes for the story and works as superb motivation for your characters as you head towards the third act.

The midpoint in *Titanic* doesn't completely derail the initial motivation of the characters, they still are in love and they still want to find a way to be together, but it has shifted and reframed their experiences and motivation due to the potential for imminent death.

A second example of an effective use of the midpoint in your story can be seen in *Captain America: The Winter Soldier*.

Throughout the first half you follow Steve Rogers as he realises he's being hunted and he begins to develop suspicions about S.H.I.E.L.D. Then, an hour and fifteen minutes in, he finds out that Hydra have infiltrated S.H.I.E.L.D. decades ago. It changes the entire conflict.

Reframing Your Story

Have your characters learn something at the midpoint, something that totally reshapes your story. Even if your characters at their core are still pursuing the same thing, it's in a different landscape with different consequences.

In *Titanic*, Jack and Rose still want to be together but now they've learned they're also sinking. In *Captain America: The Winter Soldier*, Steve still wants to find Bucky but now he's doing it having learned that Hydra have infiltrated S.H.I.E.L.D.

Writing a Clear Midpoint

When you want to write a good clear midpoint, think of it like a pivot. You build up to this revelation like one side of a triangle, then you fall back down the other side towards the climax dealing with that change that has happened.

Something to remember is that if your word count isn't putting your midpoint exactly in the middle, it really won't ruin your story. There is always flexibility with story structure so don't get too bogged down with worrying about trying to get it at exactly halfway through. But it's a good guide to try and work to for the most effective use of the midpoint.

VI
The "Three-Act Structure"

A "Three-Act Structure" is like a framework for your story, a structure to build your story around. It will move your plot along in a controlled way that keeps your story organised and making sense, with a clear beginning, middle and end. I'll be explaining what elements are included in a three-act structure, and referencing the film *Die Hard*.

What is a Three-Act Structure?

To write in a three-act structure, it's a good idea to remember this:

Act One—Put your character up a tree
Act Two—Throw stones at him/her
Act Three—Get your characters back down from the tree

It's a really effective way of understanding how to use this, and how to write within it. Die Hard is one of my favourite films, and the format is a perfect three-act structure in use:

Act One—Put John McClane up the tower
Act Two—Throw terrorists at him
Act Three—Get John McClane back down the tower

Act One

In Act One we meet John McClane, a New York City cop, who's travelled to L.A. to spend Christmas with his estranged wife, Holly, and their daughter. He goes up to the top of Nakatomi Tower to Holly's office, meets her boss and colleagues, with the Act One goal of winning back Holly's love.

We see the emerging plot for the film during Act One as the criminals break into the building whilst John and Holly and the office party are up at the top of the tower. It tells you that there will be more to this story than just John's desire to win back Holly, but John doesn't know it yet. He's just going up the metaphorical tree.

Act One ends when the terrorists announce their presence by busting into the Christmas party with their guns. That changes the story both for the audience and in terms of John McClane's goals.

Act Two

John McClane isn't with the rest of the party when the terrorists enter as he's in a bathroom having a shave in his vest. This puts him in position to spend Act Two of the movie trying to figure out how he's going to stop the terrorists, save all the party guests, and get everybody back down the tower (or the tree).

Act Two changes John's story goals from win back Holly, into save Holly, plus everybody else, and follows him on his quest to do that. We witness him fighting the terrorists and struggling to overcome the challenges they throw at him.

Act Two finishes when John McClane has weapons, a guy out front to work with, and he's ready to put his plan into action to get everybody out, and on the revelation to John McClane that Hans Gruber, the wonderful Alan Rickman, is actually the main bad guy terrorist.

Act Three

Act Three follows John McClane acting out his plan, proving to the suspicious cops outside that he's not crazy and he was right all along, and rescuing Holly. The climax draws together all the previous threads.

How to Use a Three-Act Structure

For your story, don't feel trapped by the idea of putting your character up a tree or a tower. This idea can come in so many different forms. You can do the same thing by showing your character wanting something, then learning about how to get it through experiences, and then finally going after the thing they wanted.

You can trust yourself to be creative and play with the format, rather than feeling trapped by it, but the three-act structure is a really great framework around which to base a satisfying story.

VII
How to Write Foreshadowing

Foreshadowing is the technique of hinting to your audience where your story is going, without actually telling them. It works to make your story flow and feel planned and prepared, as well as making the end feel more satisfying.

Too Much or Too Little Foreshadowing

Your use of foreshadowing needs to be subtle. Don't write hints and clues like giant arrows, pointing to the end. It needs to be done carefully. Heavy handed foreshadowing ruins the surprise and makes your story feel predictable.

Foreshadowing needs to blend into the story. Every hint you put needs to be part of the story in and of itself. If you shine a light on it so it stands out from the rest of your story unnaturally, it's too obvious. It reads like a giant sticker has been slammed onto the page saying, *"Pay attention to this!"*

However, if you use too little foreshadowing then your story will feel unprepared. Plot twists that have no foreshadowing building to their arrival feel unreal and like a last-minute plan. They don't feel real.

You need to make sure that your hints have enough of a light shone on them that when you reveal your ending, it reads to feel like you intended it from the beginning. But, despite all feeling like it's been built to, you need to surprise your audience with a sense of not seeing it coming.

Harry Potter and the Philosopher's Stone

The ending of *Harry Potter and the Philosopher's Stone* (SPOILERS) by J. K. Rowling is hinted to from the start. The moment Harry meets Professor Quirrell, the foreshadowing begins.

Professor Quirrell has the strange smelling turban, and he has been travelling recently. It is Professor Quirrell who announces the arrival of the troll. It's Professor Quirrell that Snape talked to in the forest, and Harry dreams about Professor Quirrell's turban talking to him, telling him to transfer to Slytherin.

However, all of these hints have been masked. Snape acts as the perfect red herring, and the foreshadowing blends into the rest of the story. When Quirrell is revealed to be in league with Voldemort, you're surprised, but not shocked. It makes sense. You've been led there from the beginning without realising it.

Edit It In

Editing is the perfect time to construct your foreshadowing. I wouldn't advise obsessing too heavily about foreshadowing in your first draft. Your first draft is about getting the story out and finding your ending. But once you've got to the ending, then you can go back to the beginning and lay the groundwork.

How to Write Foreshadowing

When you look at your plot twist or your climax, look at any objects, information or places that are relevant. Any weapons or tools that they need to use to accomplish their goals. Anything at all that is used in the climax needs to be present earlier in the story, so reference it but without shining a light on it.

Say your character uses a gun that was hanging on a wall, don't have them obsess for a long time about what a fascinating gun it is without context. Any observation of the gun needs to be part of a wider conversation, or a description of the room as a whole. That way, when they pick the gun up and use it at the end, your audience know it's there already. It doesn't feel like you've just shoved a gun up there last minute.

Go back through your story, and weave references to all the key information in. Allow your story to consume the hints as part of the whole, so they don't stand out, but they're still present. The first time your audience reads your story, the hints shouldn't stand out. But the second and third time, they should notice the signposts and enjoy seeing that the crafting is there from the start.

Alternatively, when you're working on your climax, pull references from the beginning of the story to use. If your character observed a gun on the wall as part of the description of the room and the people who live there, then use it. Don't invent new objects to use if you've already referenced perfectly good ones earlier in the story.

Narrative Triplets

The best and neatest foreshadowing, in my opinion, comes in the form of a Narrative Triplet. It's literally a triplet of references to something key to your story, with the final coming in the climax.

For instance, in the film *Spider-Man: Into the Spiderverse*, the three beat that builds to the climax is The Shoulder Touch. In the first instance, Uncle Aaron teaches Miles to touch a girl on the shoulder to flirt with her. In the second instance, Miles uses the shoulder touch in a failed attempt to flirt with Gwen and loses control of his powers whilst he does it. The third time he uses the shoulder touch, it's in battle against The Kingpin. He uses it with his powers successfully, and it helps him overcome The Kingpin to get victory.

The two previous uses of the shoulder touch were absorbed into the story. They made sense in the story in and of itself, without a light being shone on it to expect something later. They built the story and gave context to his relationship with both Uncle Aaron and Gwen. So, when he uses it at the end, it's even more satisfying, and makes total sense that he's got that in his toolbox of moves to use.

The Impact of Foreshadowing

By taking the time to foreshadow the end of your story, you are communicating to your audience that you have crafted this story with care. Revelations through your story that have been foreshadowed are more satisfying and make your story more entertaining.

Editing foreshadowing into your story tells your audience you knew exactly what journey you were taking them on. That you were fully in control and built this story with their pleasure in mind.

It doesn't matter that you had to go back into your story to edit it in rather than doing it from the beginning. Nobody sees that first draft but you. Your audience will benefit from the foreshadowing and effort, no matter how it got there.

VIII
The Balance Between Protagonist and Antagonist

When you're planning your story, one of the first jobs is to establish who your Protagonist and Antagonist are. Your Protagonist is your main character, the person who you are travelling with. They want something and are motivated to get it. Your Antagonist is the person who wants the opposite and is motivated to stop them. I'll be writing about the balance between them in strength, ability, and determination.

Who Is Stronger?

You move your Protagonist from passive to active at the inciting incident. That's the moment when they set out to go and get what they want, and are set in conflict with the Antagonist

If your Protagonist is stronger, and therefore more capable of succeeding than your Antagonist, it will be too easy. You want your Protagonist to have to struggle, fight, and learn. They need to be equally matched, or, ideally, outmatched.

Growing and Changing

Make your Antagonist the stronger character. When your Antagonist has a natural advantage, it forces your

Protagonist to grow and change. Every time they are blocked from achieving their goals by your Antagonist, they have to learn and adapt. It will keep the conflict alive and make your characters more interesting.

The Protagonist should only be able to succeed against the Antagonist in the climax, by using everything they've learned throughout the story.

Moana Vs Maui

In *Moana*, in order to return the heart of Te Fiti, Moana and Maui must face off against lava monster, Te Ka.

Through the course of the story, Maui acts as an Antagonist to Moana. He is stronger and more experienced than Moana and constantly tries to disrupt her on her journey. At first, Moana is no match for him. She gets trapped in a cave, she can't sail the boat alone, and she knows that without him she couldn't win.

But Moana learns. She grows and changes, and becomes equal to him, until he surrenders to her and agrees to do what she wants because she has proven herself. He then becomes an ally to her.

Moana Vs Te Ka

In facing Te Ka, Maui too must grow and change. Te Ka has long been an Antagonist to Maui, and he is frightened of her. He feels unable to face her without having control of his magic hook, but he too goes on a journey, growing and changing through the story.

At the beginning of the story, neither Moana nor Maui would be capable of standing up to Te Ka. By the end of the story, Moana is so strong and capable that she is able to part the ocean and approach Te Ka face on, returning the heart to her and turning her back into Te Fiti.

What Your Character Learns

To become capable of winning against their Antagonist, your Protagonist must learn. This could be to learn to fight and increase their strength, it could be that they learn their Antagonist's weakness and are able to use it against them, or information that allows them to win through intelligence.

The harder they have to work to get the information or ability they need, the better. The more the Antagonist blocks them and forces them to adapt, the better. At no point should your Protagonist find getting what they want easy, and at no point should they have what they need to win until the climax. Make them work for it, make them learn, make them fight.

Conflict

If at the beginning of your story your Protagonist is unable to get what they want because the Antagonist is getting in the way, your story will have conflict. Conflict is what keeps your story interesting.

By the end of the story, at cost to themselves as they have had to learn, grow, and change, your Protagonist is finally able to face the Antagonist with a chance of winning. This win should still be a challenge; don't let it become easy. Whatever it is they have learned should allow them the opportunity to win, but it shouldn't just be handed to them.

The more conflict, the bigger the struggle, the greater the challenge, the more interesting your story will be.

IX
Multiple Protagonists

The Protagonist of your story is the main character who you follow on their journey. They start the story wanting something, through the course of the story they go after it, and at the end of the story it's resolved by either getting it or not.

To be a Protagonist, they must have an Antagonist, the person or thing that is preventing them from getting what they want. Your story follows the conflict between these two characters.

When you're writing multiple protagonists, you're writing multiple people in pursuit of their goals, each with an Antagonist trying to stop them. These stories will intermingle and connect but are all their own complete conflict.

The Difference Between Ensemble and Multiple Protagonist

An ensemble cast doesn't necessarily mean you have multiple protagonists. You may have a large cast revolving around a single Protagonist, and whilst each of the characters in the ensemble is significant and motivated, they don't count as a protagonist. They're only a protagonist if you're directly following their story.

You can find examples of multiple protagonism in stories such as *The West Wing*, *Pulp Fiction*, *Lost*, and the first two *Avengers* movies, but not *Avengers: Infinity War*, because Thanos is the protagonist of that picture.

Where to Use Multiple Protagonists

A TV series is a good space for writing multiple protagonists because then your audience is able to spend more time getting to know the different characters and what they are motivated by. Over more time you can track the different characters and different stories more easily.

Films and books are harder to write a good multiple protagonist story in, simply because you have less time. You need to make sure your audience understands who all your Protagonists are and what they all want in order to tell all their stories successfully. With a more limited page count, that will be a challenge.

Be Careful with Your Structure

When you're writing a multiple protagonist story, you have to be careful to control the structure. You can end up with a bitty storyline, bobbing about so much you never fully get to grips with any of the characters' stories. Or, if you cram all the stories in, you have to race through different characters too fast, so you lose some of the details they deserve.

Whilst *Lost* is a genuinely excellent example of this style, some of the Protagonists' backstories end up cut short and rushed through. Spending too long exploring one story means you end up missing out on everybody back on the island, so something has to be sacrificed. All the characters need to have their stories moved forward in an equally interesting and developed way.

The West Wing nails multiple protagonists in a really impressive way. Aaron Sorkin, the series' genius creator, manages to make each Protagonist equally important and significant each episode. Each Protagonist has an individual story arc which is ticked along, even if it is just a small amount, each episode.

You might find that in different episodes, or different chapters, you choose to focus on one character predominantly. This allows you to develop that Protagonist without too much distraction, as happens in *Lost* and *The West Wing* for instance, but all the other characters still matter. The other storylines might not be directly involved with the focus plotline but could be thematically linked and still need to be moved forwards.

Introducing Multiple Protagonists

When you're getting to know characters in a multiple Protagonist story, you have a lot of characters to introduce with equal value quickly. You need your audience to be able to recognise who each person is, or it'll just be confusing.

If you look at how *Lost* introduces the cast, it's very clever and very effective. At first, you get to know each Protagonist based on one single thing about them, something your audience can latch on to and recognise those characters by. The "Fat Guy"—Hurly. The "Stuck Up Princess"—Shannon. The "Hero"—Jack. The "Cowboy"—Sawyer. You then slowly get to know them better, and understand what it is they want better, after you've been able to identify who each of them is.

To write this yourself, you need to give each Protagonist something really identifiable about them, something simple that isolates which character it is and can then be built from.

In *Lost*, each character is deeper and more interesting than the stereotype you're trained to recognise them by, but by having these single factors you've got a base from which to grow. Once you know who they are, you can develop them, bring in their back stories and motivations.

A way to do this well is to write your story first, then when you know your characters really well, go back and edit your first chapter. Give each Protagonist something clear that is an easy way to identify them when the audience reads their name. It's easier to do this once you've reached the end of your story and you have a full image of who the character is to extract one tiny seed from.

Emerald Wren and the Coven of Seven

For instance, in *Emerald Wren and the Coven of Seven*, I have an ensemble cast of seven. It's not a multiple Protagonist story, as Emerald is the single Protagonist, but the other six are still extremely important and motivated so I used this technique.

I went back in and made sure that early on each character had something the audience could latch onto about who they are. For example, Celeste is a Christian, and her faith is a key part of her personality and story. So, from when you first meet her, I wrote that when she's anxious she plays with her crucifix. Celeste is much more than just a Christian, but that action tells the audience something significant about her immediately that they can recall when they next read her name.

Antagonists

Every Protagonist must have an Antagonist. It could be themselves if they have internal conflict, another person in their life who wants the complete opposite to what they want, or even the world at large, nature, or society.

But to be a Protagonist they must have an Antagonist who is blocking them from getting what they want. For each of your Protagonists, you follow the conflict with the Antagonist until the climax when the conflict is resolved.

Why Write Multiple Protagonists?

The benefits of writing multiple Protagonists are that the energy of your story will be up. Every scene will have more conflict because the characters are equally important and equally motivated, and the more conflict there is in a scene, the more entertaining it is.

It isn't necessarily an easy thing to do, and won't suit every story, but if you do it well it can be very effective and entertaining.

X
Multiple Antagonists

Just as multiple Protagonist stories can be highly entertaining, stories with multiple Antagonists can work really well. However, you can write a multiple Antagonist story with just one Protagonist. Each Antagonist is set against the Protagonist in a different way, each working against what your Protagonist wants.

I'll be referencing the film *Jurassic Park*. During the course of the picture, there are multiple Antagonists all disrupting the experiences of the Protagonists, Grant, Ellie, and (essentially) the entirety of the human race. I'll explain what they do in the story, and how you can replicate that style in your own work.

Jurassic Park

The obvious antagonist in *Jurassic Park* is John Hammond. He was the designer of Jurassic Park and, arguably, is responsible for all the things that went wrong. There's also Dennis Nedry who sells the science to a rival company, then shuts down the electricity when stealing the "dino DNA", which then frees the dinosaurs from their cages. The dinosaurs themselves are also Antagonists, because they want to be free, and the humans don't want them to be free.

John Hammond

John Hammond is the "man playing God", a kind of antagonist which features frequently in stories; particularly in science fiction. Humans deciding that they are able to create and control life usually ends badly in stories, as it sets the created life against the existing life.

A lot of science fiction, at its core, is about the consequences of choosing to create sentient beings, be they living creatures or robots. The story follows the course of the human beings trying to exist, and the created life forces trying to become dominant. As their enabler, John Hammond represents the created life in this conflict.

Dennis Nedry

Dennis Nedry is representative of "the criminal". Criminals are frequently occurring Antagonists. They are morally unscrupulous characters, and their downfall is their greed. The criminal who is willing to put everyone at risk for their own personal gain is a great character to deploy in your story.

In the case of Nedry, he's there from the beginning being sneaky, and even though nobody likes him he's still trusted enough to have access to everything he needs to be the criminal. So, to use a character like this in your own story, it needs to be somebody who is motivated to put everything at risk, but also trusted enough to be able to do it. This is the character that will often be revealed as the betrayer in a plot twist moment.

Thematically Nedry is particularly interesting because he represents the lack of control John Hammond has over life. Hammond thinks he has control over everybody which is why Nedry is able to do the things he does. Hammond is arrogant enough to not consider the possibility of betrayal.

Nature

Nature itself makes an excellent antagonist in stories. As Jeff Goldblum's character Dr. Ian Malcolm says, "life will find a way."

Nature is intent on surviving and flourishing, even when humans think they are able to stop it. In *Jurassic Park*, that is demonstrated by the discovery that the dinosaurs can change their sex because of the frog DNA used in their creation. It hammers home the price of your character playing God.

Nature will not be controlled. Dinosaurs being able to change sex means they're able to breed, so they can appear in unexpected places and in larger numbers. This sometimes appears in stories in the form of a volcano, a hurricane, or a tidal wave. But the threat is always nature set to do what nature does, and humans being unable to stop it.

Antagonists vs Protagonists

Essentially, all your different Antagonists are working to do something which, when combined, cause a massive problem for your Protagonist. Individually, each Antagonist makes things a challenge, but when combined your Protagonist is outmatched and forced to grow and change.

In *Jurassic Park*, even though killing everybody isn't the goal of the Antagonists, the consequences of what they're all doing has that result.

When you have multiple Antagonists, you'll find that a number of them won't be evil, they're not a villain or a bad guy, they're just flawed humans who are unable to keep their flaws in check.

In the case of John Hammond, his flaw is his arrogance. He isn't a "bad guy" who wants to hurt people, he just lacks self-awareness and that causes him to accidentally hurt people. Personally, I really enjoy an Antagonist who is ultimately a good person but just makes huge mistakes and doesn't fix them.

What you need to remember is that when you're creating an Antagonist, their role in your story is to be Antagonistic towards your Protagonist. So, any kind of Antagonist you put into your story, there is only an Antagonist if their goals are actively set against the goals of your Protagonist.

XI
Pacing Your Story

The rate at which your plot moves forwards is referred to as the "pace" of your story. If your story has too slow a pace, it can be boring, whereas if the pace is too fast then it's unclear what's happening and why. You need to find a balance between moving forwards at the right pace, whilst still taking time to explain what is happening and why.

Conflict

To keep your story moving forwards, you always need to have active conflict in every scene. By conflict I don't mean people have to be fighting each other; nobody has the energy for constant fighting. Conflict in your scene means at no point do all your characters have what they want.

If your scene lacks conflict, if everybody has what they want, then the story won't move forwards. If people have what they want, they won't be in pursuit of anything, they won't be driving the story towards the climax. Scenes without conflict have no pace, they're stalled. The characters are just existing.

Pace Requires Conflict

Watching characters just exist isn't entertaining. You're joining these characters at this point in their lives specifically to observe their story, and if their story isn't happening, then the point of reading or watching it isn't happening either. The more conflict there is in a scene, the more characters there are in pursuit of goals, the more interesting the scene is.

To maintain the pace of your story, keep the conflicts active the whole way through your story. The conflict begins at the inciting incident, when your Protagonist goes in pursuit of their goals, up to the climax, when the character's goals are resolved.

Description

Description is what will slow the pace of your story down. If you don't describe anything in your scene then nobody will understand where they are or who they are, but if you describe so much your pace starts to crawl, your audience will get bored.

When you're focusing on description, you're less likely to be focusing on the active conflict. And, without conflict, your story slows down. So when using descriptions in your story, be considered with it and make sure you use more poetic and lengthy descriptions at points where the tension isn't too heightened, because lengthy descriptions will sap the tension you've built and ruin the scene.

Root Descriptions in Protagonist Point of View

By focusing descriptions on the character you're most interested in during the scene, you can still keep the conflict active. If your point of view character, usually the Protagonist, is personally affected by something or somebody in the scene, then they would naturally have thoughts about what they look like or what they're doing in their heads. Follow those thoughts, consider how and why those things are impacting the Protagonist, and focus descriptions on those factors.

During a big fight scene, a point of high tension, your Point Of View (POV) character would spend less time thinking about what people look like and what colour the walls are, because they'll be focussed on fighting and surviving. If your descriptions mirror that you'll have a faster pace because your scene will focus more on the conflict.

During a romantic picnic in the park, your POV character would spend more time observing the beauty of their environment, the light on the water, the smell of cut grass in the air, the way the person they're with looks at them and the way a smile plays on their lips. A slower pace will suit that scene more.

Finding the Balance

Even a slower, more ponderous scene, needs conflict. It could be internal conflict; your character isn't sure what they want or is too nervous to say something they want to say. They could have a secret or be hopeful for something to happen, like a proposal, and too scared to mention it, disappointed when it doesn't happen and struggling with their emotions.

A faster scene will still need descriptions, because if you're describing how a character is fighting another, and you don't tell your audience they were kicked in the guts, or thrown into a wall, and you don't take the time to describe how much pain they're in or how scared they are, then you'll lose the humanity.

Keeping your audience connected to the character's feelings, both in fast and slow pace scenes, keeps your audience rooted in the importance of the story. The stakes won't matter if your characters don't matter, and your characters won't matter if your audience hasn't emotionally connected to them.

XII
Avoid Writing a Passive Protagonist

One of the first rules for your Protagonist is that they should want something and, ideally, they should be wanting something they are actively in pursuit of. Being active in your story means they're taking direct action to accomplish their goals.

A passive Protagonist has things happening to them and around them. They're reacting to things, rather than pursuing something themselves. I'll be writing about why this is a problem for your story, and how to write an active protagonist.

Transitioning from Passive to Active

Your story should begin when your Protagonist transitions from passive to active. At the start of your story they're living their life but not trying to change it, then the inciting incident happens which sends them in pursuit of their goal.

That goal might be something they are setting out to accomplish or an object they want to acquire. Or, it might be when they become aware of the story antagonist and want to stop them from accomplishing their goal (such as blowing up the world if you want to go full action story).

The Problem with a Passive Protagonist

If you leave your Protagonist as passive for too long, you have no story and your audience will not connect to them. You need your audience to want to read or watch your story for its entirety, which means they have to want something for your Protagonist. If your Protagonist wants nothing, your audience will want nothing, and they'll stop caring.

When you have a passive Protagonist, bumbling from moment to moment and reacting to the things happening around them, they won't draw focus. You'll find other characters in the story are motivated, interesting, and pursuing goals which is what the passive character is bumping into. This will mean your audience will want to spend more time with them, but because you're centering the character who's doing nothing, they won't get to.

Aim to spend only a little time with your Protagonist in their passive state, just enough time that you understand *why* they become motivated.

Use the Passive State to Demonstrate Frustrations

During their passive state, show what is happening in their mundane ordinary life that is frustrating or unsatisfying. When the inciting incident happens, your audience will connect with why your Protagonist pursues their new goal.

For example, in *Lilly Prospero and the Magic Rabbit*, I spend a little time with Lilly in her passive state of going to a new school and being lonely and unhappy, wanting more from her life and longing for friendships. This means that when things change for her and she meets the talking rabbit

Jeffrey, you understand why it matters to her, and root for her to get what she wants.

The Inciting Incident

You can drop the inciting incident into the Protagonist's first scene, such as in *The Matrix*. Or you can spend a little longer with your Protagonist in their passive state such as in *Star Wars: Episode IV – A New Hope*, which sees Luke Skywalker stuck on Tatooine staring at the two suns and feeling like he wants more. There is no definite right way or wrong way, and we can all have our own personal style, as long as you do send your Protagonist on a journey.

There's a reason you're piggybacking on that Protagonist at that point in their life, and it's not to watch them living their ordinary life and doing nothing noteworthy. That's boring. That's not a story. You're on their shoulder for their life *now* because of the active goal they're pursuing.

XIII
Making Your Characters Distinct

When you're writing lots of different characters, it's quite easy to fall into the trap of making all your characters be different versions of yourself. They might look different and have different goals, but their personalities blur into one another and their speech patterns are identical, so it ends up reading like you're having conversations with yourself. I'll be explaining why writing distinct characters is important, and techniques you can use to do it well.

Different Personalities Make Your Story Interesting

If everybody is essentially the same person, and talks in the same way, there will be no natural conflict in the conversation, and conflict is what makes the story interesting.

It is always more entertaining and interesting to have multiple personalities on the page or screen. There will be friendly people, aggressive people, shy people and confident people. If they have negative behaviour patterns it leaves room for growth and change. A story arc where you follow a character's development always makes them more entertaining to read or watch.

If you're writing an ensemble cast, it is especially important to make your characters distinct, and also an easier trap to fall into to not doing so.

You're trying to balance multiple motivations and activities as well as your main plot, and the conversation style of the characters becomes less important and those characters all become variants on the same person. For you, it makes the job easier, for your audience, it makes it dull because the story will lack drama.

Develop Different Personalities

When you start creating your character personalities, it's important to remember that you don't have to *like* all your characters. This is something I personally struggled with when I started out. I wasn't good at writing characters who, unless they were a clear villain, behaved in ways I didn't like or wasn't comfortable with.

Good characters can make bad choices and do things that you personally wouldn't do. Your characters are not part of you, make them free to do things that you wouldn't do, things that you don't like, and they won't all be carbon copies of you.

Pose a Moral Dilemma

One way to do this is, is to imagine your collection of characters standing together and pose a question to them. Something complex, such as a moral question or a political one, and work out how each of the characters would respond. In a room full of people, you're going to get a room full of opinions. Some will agree on some points, disagree on others, but there will be different opinions.

Then work out *how* your characters reply. Are they confident or are they shy? Do they try to dominate the debate? Are they reasonable or hostile, are they willing to change their mind with argument or are they steadfast?

The way they respond, and what they respond with, demonstrates their personality. Carry that throughout your story in how they respond to any scenario you put them in, and they'll keep that distinct character trait that you want.

Conflict Between Characters

Once you've got these clear and distinct personalities, it's easy to play with them. You can add conflict on a scene level through disagreements or misunderstandings, or just making someone in that scene uncomfortable with a character's responses to a scenario.

Conflict is essential for making your story interesting and it will bring your story alive. Even a simple question between friends in a scene of "what should we do tonight?" opens up possibilities for a range of opinions with fallout from the conversation.

Once you've established character personalities, you can challenge your characters to change, you can show layers. Perhaps your initially hostile and abrasive character has a vulnerable side, damage in their past that makes them behave that way when challenged. Allowing for change and layers in your diverse characters makes them more interesting and human.

Flaws Make Characters Relatable

The more human your characters are, the more relatable they are, and even if you don't agree with everything a character does (and a flawless character is boring), you and your audience will find a way to connect with them when you show multiple facets of their personalities.

XIV
Writing Flawed Characters

When you write a story, quite often you'll find that you will write your Protagonist to be an essentially "perfect" human. They don't make mistakes, they don't make bad decisions, they don't do things wrong. Your Protagonist will interact with bad people and flawed people surrounding them, but they themselves are flawless. The problem is, if your main character is perfect, they'll be boring, and they'll be unrelatable.

The Problem with Writing Perfect People

Your Protagonist is who your audience will be riding along with, the person who they need to connect with and understand, as they move through your story. If your Protagonist is so flawless that your audience cannot relate to them or understand them, then you will lose your audience.

It's important to remember that everybody makes mistakes. Everybody does bad things and then lives in regret and learns from it. Everybody is carrying damage and scars that cause us to behave in ways that can hurt others. Our damage and our flaws are part of our humanity, and if you're representing a character that is allegedly human but carries none of these flaws with them, then they will not read as human and your audience will not connect with them as human. They'll be more interested in and connected to the peripheral characters who are carrying all these flaws, and who we can see ourselves in.

The Writer's Vanity Project

The other problem with writing a perfect character is it can come across as a vanity project. When you read or watch a story about a perfect person, it's easy to assume that the writer, that's you, is trying to represent all the bits they love about themselves and turn them into a person.

Male filmmakers who make action movies about flawless heroes who can tackle a romantic relationship as easily as they can defuse a bomb are particularly guilty of this.

Popular Perfect Characters

The only thing to counter this argument is the popularity of characters such as Superman and Captain America. If you think about the negative response from the DC fandom to Superman breaking Zod's neck in *Man of Steel*, it shows the commitment the fans have to keeping Superman as this flawless angelic figure. Captain America is also perfect. Even when the situation is complicated and other characters disagree with him, such as in *Captain America: Civil War*, you can see that Captain America is always trying to make the right choice for the right reasons. Even if you disagree with the choices he's made, they're not made out of selfishness or evil.

People get tired and stressed, and all the energy we spend trying to be the best versions of ourselves gets drained, and that's when our bad sides are more likely to come out. That's when we're likely to snap, and that's when we're likely to make mistakes. If you are writing a character, in the style of Superman or Captain America, who never gets tired and drained, then it makes sense that they'll never get so tired that their dark side is able to come out.

As I say, the popularity of these characters counters my argument, but personally I find Superman and Captain America to be some of the least interesting characters.

Your Audience Might Feel Alienated

If you do choose to write a flawless character, for whatever reason, perhaps the important thing to consider is your audience. A superhero fandom might embrace a flawless character, but if you're writing a story about a mother, you're less likely to find audience sympathy.

If I read a book about a mother who is perfect, always calm, never shouts, never cries, I am going to feel irrationally angry about that character and not connect with her at all. I will be unlikely to finish that book because it won't read as real to me.

However, if you write a story about a mother who sometimes struggles, and worries, and gets frustrated, and can't always sit on the floor playing for hours, then I will be right there and invested and caring about her enough to follow her story to the end. And making your audience care enough about your Protagonist so that they stick around is the name of the game.

In a similar way, if you're writing for teenagers and you write a teen who is always making good choices and doesn't screw up, your teenage readers won't understand them because teenagers are always struggling with life and making mistakes along the way.

Flaws Allow Us to Learn

The arc your character goes on, from making mistakes to learning and improving, is an interesting and exciting part of a story. If your story starts with a perfect character, be they an action hero, mother, or teenager, then where can they go? They have nothing to learn. The character arc is far more interesting as they become better people, than just seeing them perfect in the beginning, and staying consistent and unchanged by your story to the end.

XV
Motivating Your Villains

When you're writing a story, it's obviously important to make sure your Protagonist is well motivated. However, if your Antagonist isn't motivated equally, and exists solely to disrupt life for your Protagonist, your story will lack depth.

Considering your Antagonist to be the Protagonist in their own story will mean you make your Antagonist an interesting and complex character, which in turn will improve the quality of your story. I'll explain how to motivate your villains well and give examples from *Dr. Horrible's Sing-Along Blog*.

Antagonists are Still Human

Depending on the kind of story you're writing, your Antagonist could be motivated to come between your Protagonist and their love interest, or to blow up the world, but whatever it is that makes them the villain of your story, make sure you motivate their behaviour on a human level, make it something real and understandable.

To find the human motivation at the core of even the dastardliest villainous crimes, you should be able to journey back in time to the base of their motivation which can come from a place of good. That good can, over time, become warped and twisted as the villain makes bad decisions and becomes corrupted, but at the very base of their crimes is a desire to improve something either in their life or their world.

I'm referring to the Antagonist and the villain of your story as if they're the same person here, and for the most part that's likely to be the case. However, it's not necessarily true. The Antagonist is whoever, or whatever, is set against your Protagonist, whereas the villain is someone who wants to do villainous things

Dr. Horrible's Sing-Along Blog

A great example to check out for how to do this well is in *Dr. Horrible's Sing-Along Blog*. The reason it's such a great example is because the villain is actually the Protagonist, which is very unusual, but works very well.

Because Dr. Horrible is the Protagonist, the writers Joss, Jed and Zack Whedon, and Maurissa Tancharoen, have made sure you sympathise with him and want good things for him. You cannot sympathise with a villain if their motivation isn't understandable and doesn't come from somewhere good. The Antagonist, Captain Hammer, is actually the hero.

Dr. Horrible wants to do evil things, and this is made clear immediately. There's no confusion over the fact he's a villain. He wants to join the "Evil League of Evil", admission to which is dependent on his willingness to commit murder; and he wants to use his Freeze Ray to freeze people and disrupt the progress of society.

On the surface, his doesn't sound like a character you should find endearing or root for, which makes him a challenging Protagonist. Partly this works because of the natural charm that Neil Patrick Harris brings to the role, and that shouldn't be overlooked; however, with the writing of that character, Tancharoen and the Whedon brothers give him humanity and vulnerability.

Give Your Villain Things They Care About

To make his motivations come from a place of good, Dr. Horrible is shown despairing over the negative parts of our society and he is driven to improve our world. This sounds like a noble and honest pursuit. He talks about wanting to change the problem of homelessness from the root rather than by just patching it by raising money with Penny, the love interest. However, his efforts are ultimately broken by his own characters flaws, and it's his devotion and love for Penny which both brings the optimism for the character to have a happy ending, and his ultimate downfall.

Giving your villain things that they care about and things that they love, such as Dr. Horrible's love for Penny, demonstrates their humanity and the fact they're driven by more than just villainy. Make sure that their desire to do evil or disrupt the good guy's life is just one aspect of a rich and developed personality.

Find the Humanity

Even the most terrible villains have come from somewhere; even the most violent of criminals have passions and interests, and most bad guys have been corrupted and twisted into doing bad things rather than setting out initially to be bad. Representing that in your story will make it a richer experience, and also show a better understanding of humanity that your audience will connect

XVI
Show Don't Tell

Show don't tell is a piece of writing advice that is regularly given to writers, but without development it can be hard to understand. I previously wrote about showing not telling your character's environment and actions, but for this I'll be focusing on what show don't tell means in relation to your characters emotions and feelings.

What Does Show Don't Tell Mean?

If you want to tell your readers how a character feels, you can say words like "scared" or "passionate" or "angry" and it will very quickly and efficiently tell your readers what feelings the character has. It works but it's dry, it's flat, and it doesn't build the connection between your reader and your character.

Pushing your readers inside your character's mind by showing how those emotions are making them behave is stronger, it's more interesting, and it makes your reader feel what your character feels.

By showing not telling, you make your readers feel that the story is woven intrinsically to the character, rather than being an outside observer simply being told what's going on.

Body Language

Whilst we all understand what it means to feel angry, when you're connected to the interiority of the angry person by their body language, you really feel it with them.

An angry person will clench their fists, set their jaw, feel bubbling fury in their guts that threatens to erupt out of them. They'll try to control their words, their voice will shake as they try not to shout, but they won't be able to control it any longer and they'll yell everything they're angry about directly at the person whom they're angry with.

Being told they're angry might make sense, and logically you'll understand why they've shouted, but the build-up, and body language and feelings inside, really make you part of that anger.

Writing Interiority

If you're sticking to one point of view character in the scene, as you should, you'll be able to give their interiority as they talk to people, and how they interpret how other people talk to them.

If your character fancies someone, when that person speaks you could tell your audience that they are giggling. Or you could follow your character's interiority, how their heart is fluttering, and hands are sweating, how they're trying not to be silly but can feel themselves giggle because of being overcome by emotions. You can talk about how they move their eyes up and down him, absorbing the shape of his body, his firm arms, solid chest, up to his beautiful soft eyes with just a hint of mischief.

As the character who is the object of desire speaks, your character will be listening for clues as to whether the attraction is mutual, hints of flirtation, hoping to interpret those signs right and nervous they'll get it wrong. There will be anxiety and hope mingling together causing butterflies in their chest.

Again, putting your audience inside your character responding to a person make it feel real. The interaction suddenly becomes more real and that passion and attraction feels part of the story in a richer way, rather than just being told that your character is attracted to someone.

Make Your Readers Feel

I've written before about how if you can connect your audience to your characters strongly enough, you'll be able to make them cry when you throw tragedy into the story. Be it a broken heart from the loss of a lover, or the death of a loved one, using the technique of show don't tell for those feelings will help your quest to use that bond to make your reader cry.

Most of us have had our hearts broken, had someone we love betray us, and we know what it feels like. If you tell your readers that your character is grieving a lost relationship, it will make sense and their tears won't be confusing. But reliving those feelings through the character, experiencing their pain with them, will mean you're not only feeling their pain but feeling your own heartache all over again.

Dig deep into your own experiences, your own pain, and bleed it onto the page. Write their feelings as they swarm through their body, the loss of the future they had so believed in, the sickness at never holding that person again.

Write the feeling of burning on their skin from the last time they felt their lover's touch, how they want to throw up and scream and cry all at the same time. The abject misery and despair of losing that person you'd given your body, your trust, and your future to.

Write it and feel it as you write it. If you feel it, your readers will feel it. If your readers feel it, then that character is now part of them.

Connecting Your Readers to Your Characters

Showing how your character feels draws your readers in and makes your characters feel like people they're bonded to and can relate to on a deeper and more meaningful level.

When your readers can relate to your characters and feel part of their story, everything in your story will become more real and matter more to them. If it matters, they'll be invested and want to stick around to the end, read further adventures if you write a sequel, and care enough about your characters to leave good reviews.

XVII
World Building

World Building is the technique of telling your readers what world your story is set in, whether the laws of nature match ours, whether there is magical lore they need to understand, and how the society functions. World Building is essential for most stories, otherwise your readers won't understand how your characters function throughout the story, but it can be done badly. I'll explain about how to World Build effectively, and mistakes to avoid.

Stories in Our World

If you're setting your story in present day, and in the world as it is now, your world building will be minimal compared to a high fantasy story. However, you'll still need to establish anything relevant to your story.

If the story requires reference to politics, what political party is in power. If your story talks about travelling overseas, then any travel restrictions or international conflict may be relevant. However, for the most part, if you're telling a story set in our world with characters that abide by our laws, then you don't need to tell your audience much for it to make sense.

Urban Fantasy Stories

For an urban fantasy story, you first need to establish that it is our world, but it is enhanced by magic. I write urban fantasy, so in *Lilly Prospero and the Magic Rabbit* I begin the story in the mundane world of a standard British school. Lilly has lessons, interacts with other children, gets told off by teachers. It rapidly feels like the experiences most people in our world can relate to.

Once you've established that your urban fantasy is in our world, you'll need to introduce the concept of magic. You can do this in one giant crash bang, if your characters are all familiar with the magic, or more gently by explaining there is magic to someone unaware.

In *Buffy the Vampire Slayer*, Buffy is the character already familiar with the magic in that world and must explain it to Xander and Willow who are unaware. This gives you both the sensation of the world existing prior to the story, and a way of introducing the concept of the lore in that world to both the audience and the new characters.

High Fantasy

High Fantasy stories are set in worlds entirely different to ours. It could be in space, such as aboard Serenity in *Firefly*, or a fantasy realm, such as Westeros in *Game of Thrones*, but it's somewhere where everything is different and needs to be learned by your audience.

In a High Fantasy story, you won't have characters unaware of the world to explain it to, like you do in *Buffy the Vampire Slayer*, so you have to begin your story already entrenched in the world as it is. This requires world building that is more baked into the way you tell your story, and it has to be done carefully to avoid info dumping, which is boring and will boot your audience out.

In *Star Wars: Episode IV – A New Hope*, the world building is just part of the story, and you learn what's going on by following the course of the story and, even though it's an unfamiliar world, you become absorbed into it and it still makes sense. In *The Lord of the Rings*, more care is taken to explain the history of the rings and the realms, and why everything is the way it is before you try and follow Frodo on his quest.

Sloppy World Building

If you are not clear about the magical lore or the way your world functions, then you will write it in a way that is unclear, which will mean your audience doesn't understand it either. If something has been established as a truth in your world and then, later, you change it a little because it's inconvenient to the story right now, that is sloppy world building.

For instance, referencing *Buffy the Vampire Slayer* again, in season one it's established that vampires can't come out in the day because the sunlight kills them. They live in nests, multiple vampires usually in a crypt or abandoned warehouse, and they stay out of the way until sundown.

However, through the course of the show this changes. Vampires can go out in the daylight as long as they cover up with a heavy coat. Vampires can drive during the day as long as the windows of the car are *mostly* painted black with only streaks of sunlight getting in to show them where to go. It appears that sunlight is less dangerous than it's first written to be.

Sloppy world building tells your audience that you don't really know what's going on, and it tells your audience that whatever they think they know about the world they're experiencing could change. If the world can change without warning, you can't count on anything being as important as you think it is, the dangers can be different, and the threat levels can change. How tense are you supposed to be at any given moment if the rules can change depending on what works for that particular part of the story?

How to World Build

Establishing the world your story is in needs to happen relatively quickly in your story. If you're telling urban fantasy, let your audience know that there is magic in the first act and hint at the potential for it before the end of the first act. If you're telling high fantasy, they'll know immediately it's not their world, but you'll need to explain enough about the world they're in that the story makes sense faster.

If you're able to use an entry point character, somebody who is from outside and coming in, then you can explain to your audience at the same time as you explain to the character. In high fantasy, that could be someone from a different area of the world to the one your story is set in, such as The Shire, or it could be somebody training up to be a powerful wizard who needs educating.

If you can, just let your story happen and explain along the way as the story needs it. In *Firefly* you're thrown right into Mal and the crew's exploits onboard Serenity. You learn about The Alliance as it becomes relevant when Simon and River come aboard.

Keep It Interesting

World building can be a tedious experience that your audience has to get through in order to get to the actual story. If you integrate the world and the lore into your plot in a way that intrigues your audience, you can make it something they're eager to learn, rather than a duty to endure.

At the beginning of *Star Wars: Episode I – The Phantom Menace*, you have two Jedi discussing politics and trade unions over tea. It establishes something important about why the story goes the way it does, and what the active conflict in that world is, but it's incredibly dull.

Compare that with when Daenerys steps into the fire with her dragon eggs in *Game of Thrones*. That moment establishes the changing circumstances for dragons in that world and that her family bloodline cannot be killed by fire and is an incredibly important piece of world building. But it's also exciting and dramatic, it draws the audience in.

World Building Through Characters

To world build as your story goes, rather than with an info dump or an entry point character, you need to ground your story firmly in the characters more so than the world they're living in. Root your story in who they are, what they want, and how they're going about getting it and let the world be peripheral to that.

Keeping your fantasy story focused on the characters allows the world to take form around them, to come clear to your audience, as the people they're invested in react to things around them. Because it's the humanity in the people you're invested in, the world building can come second and happen more gradually. Good characterisation is essential to make that work though, you have to make your audience care about those characters, and you have to make them care fast.

Keep the Rules Clear and Consistent

If in your first draft, the rules you've established for your world take a wander, it's fine. First drafts are messy and that's normal, but then you have to edit, and you have to edit well.

Make a decision and stick to it, what magic is there, how does it work, what can vampires do, what laws of nature control your characters actions? If there is anywhere in your story that it's unclear, sharpen it and make sure your audience can latch onto exactly what happens in the world they're reading, don't leave it messy.

If you're writing a series, either of books or films, or a TV Show, and you find later on that you do need to adapt some of the rules you've established for your world, then try and find a way to explain it. Something has changed, something fundamental to the world they're in, and the characters are adapting to those changes as the audience is.

Pulling a switcheroo on your audience, changing things without explaining why, and having your characters react as if nothing has changed, is sloppy and makes the rest of your story unconvincing. Anything can be changed as long as you give a reason for it and have your characters react accordingly.

XVIII
How to Write Flashbacks

Flashbacks in your story are where you have two timelines, your main story line, and then a storyline in the past where you discover your character's history. At points during the plot, you flashback to the historical timeline for a scene or two, before returning to the present.

Why Use Flashbacks?

Flashbacks are used to explain situations in the present day by taking the audience into the character's memories. They let you witness key events in character backstory that impacts how they're behaving, or events in the past that are shaping present day politics.

Flashbacks are a great way of using the show don't tell rule to literally show the audience why things are happening. Rather than having a character give an "as you know" type info dump to another character which is boring and tedious, you actually get to witness the action.

Avoid Breaking the Tension

Disrupting the flow of your main story to show sequences in a non-linear style can boot your audience out of the story by breaking the tension you've been building in one timeline, because you have to go elsewhere.

To avoid breaking the tension with flashbacks, make the scenes in the past somewhere the audience wants to go. Withhold certain key information from your reader, information they want to learn, and promise that the answers will be found in the flashbacks.

By using the flashbacks to support and boost the present-day storyline by providing interesting answers, it builds up the excitement of the present-day timeline rather than distracting from it.

To promise your audience an exciting thread of information in the flashbacks, you need to tease your audience. Build questions in their minds, about a mysterious past or significant event, that they want to go and find out about.

The Past Must Support the Present

If you just go into the past to show events that you find interesting, but that don't support and enhance your main storyline, you're focusing on what you want and ignoring what your audience wants. And they will feel that.

If you particularly enjoy writing the scenes in the past, you have to either create a reason to go back there by placing key information there that your audience needs to know, or, if you've run out of reasons to go back, just accept that your time in the past is over.

How I Wrote Flashbacks

I wrote flashbacks as a key part of my third novel *Emerald Wren and the Coven of Seven*. I found that teasing the audience with the past of Emerald and Maram's life, and how they got to where they are in the present-day story, worked well.

I used the flashbacks to both build the mystery of the two women and their lives and resolve and explain mysteries in the present day. Whilst I really enjoyed writing about their lives growing up, I had to stop jumping into the past when everything that needed explaining from that timeline had been completed.

Lost

I'm a fan of how flashbacks are used in the TV series *Lost*. The flashbacks build intrigue about the characters; you get just enough to tell you a bit about who they are and what their secrets are, but not so much that the character loses their intrigue.

The drip feeding of information through these flashbacks is what keeps the audience wanting to go back there. It's just enough information each time that you're satisfied, and it contributes to the main story, but not so much that you've done it all and have no reason to flashback again.

Arrow

If you run out of information to give in the past, your audience won't want to bother going back there, and if your audience doesn't want to go back there you shouldn't bother writing back there.

For instance, in *Arrow*, the writers kept doing flashbacks to the island where Oliver Queen was stranded, and they distracted from the main storyline. Because it had been established that the show's format included flashbacks, despite running out of storylines on the island, they had to make it increasingly ridiculous to try and justify going back there.

Linking the flashbacks to the present-day timeline wasn't very well done, and I found present day *Arrow* was the story I wanted, the flashbacks were what I had to endure. Ultimately, that's why I fell off and stopped watching. The show is very popular and successful, but I feel that that's *despite* the use of flashbacks, rather than because of them. Whereas in *Lost*, I feel the flashbacks were a massive factor in its success.

Remember to Keep Flashbacks Intriguing

If you want to write flashbacks, remember to keep your audience interested in the past timeline by using it to boost the intrigue of the present-day storyline. In the flashbacks, thread little pieces of information that add to and enhance the character and the plot rather than distracting from it.

XIX
"Narrative Triplets"

A "Narrative Triplet" is a story tool that you can use to make you story progress and keep it interesting. When a Narrative Triplet is used it makes the story feel carefully constructed, and makes the climax extremely satisfying for the audience.

I'll explain what a Narrative Triplet is, give you examples of one in use, and explain how to replicate the technique in your own writing.

Joker

To explain the concept of the Narrative Triplet, I'll be referencing scenes from the 2019 movie *Joker*, so if you haven't seen it this will contain spoilers.

When Jonathan and I saw *Joker*, we saw this Narrative Triplet coming because it was so beautifully set up, and once you're aware of them and understand them you'll start to spot them in stories too. But spotting them doesn't take away the pleasure. I actually really enjoy it because I appreciate the effort that has gone into the composition.

The Staircase – 1

In *Joker*, there's a sequence in the first act of the film where Arthur Fleck is walking up a staircase. in the city after having been to see his therapist. He has explained about his journal and been to collect his drugs, and he is trudging up this stairway between buildings. Its grungy and dark. It feels oppressive.

The character is clearly in a dark place, he is depressed and struggling. The staircase represents the challenge he is facing just to move through his life.

The Staircase – 2

The staircase appears for the second time in the middle of the film. This time it is right after he has been fired from his job, and he is really struggling with his illness and his life. Walking up those stairs is even harder.

The weight on his shoulders is even harder to cope with. He is hunched and dragging himself. Getting up those stairs is clearly a physical and mental struggle for him.

The effort to get up those stairs a second time is a clear demonstration of the escalation in his terrible circumstances. The first time was hard, the second time is harder.

The Staircase – 3

The third time the staircase is used is at the end of the film. Whereas previously he was moving up the stairs, in the third appearance he is coming down the stairs, dressed in full Joker outfit and make up. This time he is dancing.

He is light, and easily descends the stairs without effort. The scene is brighter than in the previous two, and he has lost the hunched shoulders and haggard expression. It's the opposite of the previous two appearances.

At this point, he has killed his mother, he has killed the man who gave him the gun, and he has embraced this darkness inside him. This has freed him.

Flipping the staircase scene around from the previous two instances, and having him dance down the stairs, demonstrates the change in his emotional state. It makes for a very satisfying visual contrast.

How to Write a Narrative Triplet

If you want to use the technique of the Narrative Triplet in your story, the best way to do it is to start at the end and back edit. If you write something in at the end of your story that makes a beautiful representation of your character's new state, you can go in and insert the previous two instances into the first and second act.

The important thing to remember is that the first two are different to the third, demonstrating a change in your character's state. The first instance sets the tone, the second is an escalation of the first. The third then reverts it to show the change.

So, in *Joker*, the first act shows his state, he's depressed and tired. In the second act he's struggling more, it's harder and more painful for him. In the third act he has been freed. He is light and dancing down.

Why Use a Narrative Triplet?

Taking the time to put the Narrative Triplets in makes the third instance extremely satisfying. You are able to demonstrate the emotional state of your character, their new circumstances or the lessons they've learned. It makes for a really satisfying ending and rewards your audience for paying attention.

Whilst each instance would work alone and tell you something about your character and what's happening in their life, the Narrative Triplet ties a bow on your story. It makes the story feel composed, and the climax a better experience.

XX
Deaths of Main Characters

If you're writing a book or script where there is risk or peril, and you want your audience to believe in it and feel tense during scenes with fights or danger, you need to be willing to kill your main characters. But killing them needs to be done in a way that actually causes the sense of tension you need your audience to feel. I'll explain how to kill your main characters in the most effective way for your story.

Character Deaths Build Tension

If you kill characters to create that sense of tension and fear, but only kill side characters or characters you have introduced clearly with the sole purpose of killing them, you will do nothing to build suspense or a sense of danger. Your audience will simply not go with you on that emotional journey and will therefore be outside of your story and less invested.

This is a frequently occurring problem in series. It's natural that if you've set up a group of characters that you love writing, and you've built a whole world for them to have adventures in, that you want to keep those characters alive so you can keep telling those stories.

However, if your gang of main characters is going into frequent dangerous situations where you want your audience to be scared or worried for them, and time after time they magically survive, your series will lack impact.

Write Them to Die

To avoid it feeling like nobody important will ever die—and if you struggle with getting so emotionally attached to your characters that you can't kill them—design a character with the intent of writing their death. But don't make it obvious to your audience, because if they read like they were written to die then their death won't carry any weight because everybody will see it coming.

Surprising your audience with the death of a character is the way to shatter the expectation that everybody is safe because they're the main characters, so when you write your character to kill them, write them as if you have a whole journey ahead of them planned out.

Write a plot and character as dynamic and complex and motivated as your other characters, with hopes and dreams and goals, and write them going for what they want with the same enthusiasm as you write your surviving characters. There should be no sign in the way that character comes across that you're building to their death, because then when you kill them and their journey is cut short, their story is left unfinished and that is the shock.

Make Your Audience Worry

By using your audience's intuition about where a character's story is going against them, and cutting it short without any kind of conclusion for that character, you make it feel like nobody is safe and your audience feel the sense of danger you want them to have.

Once the supposedly safe character has been killed, your audience will go into any future battle or danger scene with the uncertainty of who will survive. You have immediate suspense and tension, and your audience will have a better and more exciting experience of your story.

Of course, certain stories do this with more vigour than others. Nobody lacks for fear that somebody might die when reading or watching *Game of Thrones,* but it can almost have the opposite effect.

If you're constantly waiting for the next person to die, then you're expecting it, which means it will be less of a gut punch. Whilst it has the impact of making your audience believe that the peril is real, I personally enjoy a little more shock factor. I enjoy character deaths that are surprising, because they have more of an emotional impact on the story and audience than if everybody is just waiting for it to happen.

TV and Film are Different

The process of writing TV shows and film series is different to that of writing a book, because you have contracts with working actors. So, killing a character comes with extra issues, such as potentially firing someone; but in a book series you don't have that problem.

Alternatively, you might have to write an unintended death scene due to an actor becoming unavailable for some reason. So be prepared for screenwriting to carry different issues to navigate with deaths of characters than with books.

XXI
Character Backstory

Your character's backstory is their history and life prior to your jumping in point for this story. I'll explain how much backstory you should give to your characters, how much you should make present in your plot, and how much you should prepare rather than find out and fill in along the way according to what is useful to the story and character as you go.

Writing Backstory in Advance

An argument for writing a lot of backstory in advance of telling your story is that you'll go in with a full and rounded understanding of your characters. You can send them into situations and conflict knowing you can make their behaviour consistent and not accidentally break their character by having them react strangely because it suits the moment rather than the character as a whole.

A solid backstory will also help ensure each character is unique and has a layered motivation which makes them a far more dynamic and interesting character to read.

The better you know and understand who your character is, and why, the more convincing you can make that character be.

Don't Overload Your Story

If you have a lot of character backstory already plotted, it can be tempting to overload it on your story. An info dump of backstory makes for dull reading and can distract from forming opinions on them as new people and how they are in the present day.

If you go in fresh and discover who they are along the way, you can fill in backstory, such as a troubled childhood or bad relationship, as it suits your story now. That will then shape their behaviour and be interesting, but only comes out when it's actually relevant and interesting rather than crowbarring it in just because it's there in your head and you've created it, so you don't want to waste it.

You Might Feel Trapped by Backstory

Another problem with writing too much backstory in advance is you might feel trapped by it. If you are telling your story and you find you are going in a slightly different direction than you expected, or you think of an interesting plot development as you write, but find that the backstory you've so meticulously created for that character doesn't suit, then you can feel unable to explore that idea, and thus be restricted in your creativity.

If you've not gone too deep into their character prior to telling the story, you can grow them as you write, and find reasons and ways to follow the ideas you have without limitation.

Backstory Demonstrates Humanity

That said, if your character has no history, and no scars and damage from their past, then they're going to be flat and uninteresting. So, whether the backstory is part of what you've prepared, or it's discovered along the way to suit your story, revealing it an interesting way is the key to writing a successful character.

Integrating backstory in an interesting way can be done in a variety of ways. Flashbacks are a way of taking your audience with your character to experience those key events in their life directly, or by how they react to circumstances in the present day that reveals something about who they are.

A common trope for revealing backstory through interactions is the "bad boy with a heart of gold", who treats his girlfriend terribly, but has a lot of scarring and damage from his past that he slowly reveals, that makes the audience sympathetic to him, and gives her motivation to stick around and support him. Showing how a bad character got that way in their backstory, how the bullied becomes the bully, is a way of humanising an Antagonist and creating a layered and interesting character.

It's a really good way of developing a character because first you learn about who they are now, and then you learn how they got that way. It doesn't overload your audience, but it does help build the relationship between character and audience.

Make Sure Your Audience Wants It Before You Reveal It

Ultimately, it's important to remember that you shouldn't reveal character backstory to your audience until they care enough about that character to want to learn it. If you start shoving backstory into your plot before your audience cares, it's overloading and off-putting, and if you include backstory that is irrelevant to who that character is now and the story you're telling, nobody will care, and your readers or viewers will get bored.

When your audience has developed feelings of either positivity or negativity towards your character, you can either develop and intensify, or challenge those feelings, by revealing backstory. It makes your characters deeper and more interesting, and your audience will become more emotionally invested and care more about what happens to those characters. But if you heap paragraphs of backstory in that don't move the plot forwards, just keep the characters in the same place whilst giving the audience a history lesson, your story will feel stagnant.

XXII
Writing Natural Dialogue

When you're writing dialogue in your story, try and make sure it reads like people actually speak, rather than reading like it was written. Dialogue that reads like it's artificial will make your characters feel artificial, and they'll be harder to connect with on a human level. I'll explain techniques you can use to make sure your dialogue reads as both natural, and entertaining.

Natural Dialogue Doesn't Mirror Real Speech

For a story, natural dialogue must be easy to say out loud, and should flow in a comfortable way. However, natural dialogue in real life includes a lot of ums and erms, sentences that sometimes get lost, and repetition of words when thoughts are being gathered.

Natural dialogue in real life will not have the bookending of thoughts that you might craft for your scene, jokes that are carefully set up through the character interactions foreshadowing for events to come in the future, or the scene-level narrative triplets that make reading that scene so satisfying.

You don't go into a conversation in real life making a point, which you then repeat halfway through, and then conclude at the end with either opinions meeting or minds changed, but for a story that's watched or read, that is very satisfying.

When you're writing natural dialogue, you're not actually attempting to mirror human speech. Your job is to write perfectly crafted speech that, essentially, tricks your audience into believing it's natural.

Sorkinian Dialogue

The TV series *The West Wing* is a perfect example of dialogue that is both very natural, but also beautifully composed. The characters speak incredibly quickly, the scenes have bounce and are entertaining whilst delivering information both to the other characters and the audience, in a speedy and easy-to-follow way. There are narrative triplets, jokes, foreshadowing, and references to previous scenes woven into the speech.

Nobody naturally speaks in that way, but the scenes still come across as natural because the words being used are very normal, and they're not being forced to try and use sentences that don't flow in a human way. When you can see actors trying to force lines out that don't flow naturally, it's very obvious.

Say Lines Out Loud

When you write your dialogue, try saying it out loud. Even if you're writing a conversation to be read not spoken, your readers will get stuck on that conversation if their brains won't naturally say it. It boots them out.

Read your speech out loud, try and say it quickly and normally, and if you find yourself getting stuck or stumbling over the words you've chosen, it needs changing.

Find alternative words or speech patterns that can be spoken more easily.

It's worth noting that for musicals or high fantasy stories, your dialogue will not be particularly natural because of the context. People don't naturally sing their conversations, and if you're writing elves and warlocks in a mysterious far away fantasy land, they are unlikely to speak like a couple going out for drinks in modern day Britain. Find the natural style for your specific genre, but still make sure you can say it with ease.

Fake It to Make It

Part of the magic of storytelling is tricking your audience into believing that human beings would communicate in that way. That's one of the reasons musicals can be off-putting for some people, because nobody would *actually* burst into song in that manner.

The fact that nobody would *actually* speak in the carefully crafted manner in which scenes are arranged in books or dramas is irrelevant, because they've been tricked into believing it's possible because the words and flow have been written to sound natural. If those scenes were written how human beings actually speak, they'd realise they prefer crafted speech!

XXIII
The Lie Your Protagonist Believes

Giving your Protagonist an interesting arc where they grow and change as a person is an important part of storytelling. If they come out of the story unchanged and having learned nothing, there is no point in sending them on that journey in the first place.

The lie your Protagonist believes takes your character at the start of your story, where they will believe something about themselves and the world they live in, and follows them through the course of the story as they learn the truth. I'll be writing about what effect it has on your story, how to write it into your own work, and referencing *The Nightmare Before Christmas*.

What is the Lie?

The lie the Protagonist believes can be something external about the world, but more often it is likely to be something internal about themselves. They believe they want or need something to be happy, and are motivated to get it, but through the story they realise that it's not true.

You see this a lot in romantic comedies where the girl believes she's in love with one man, and through the course of the story it turns out she's in love with somebody else. However, the example I'm going to write about is Jack Skellington.

Jack Skellington

In *The Nightmare Before Christmas*, Jack Skellington sings a song about how bored he is of being the king of Halloween, and how he longs to be anything else. He believes that his happiness will be found somewhere else.

He then discovers Christmas Town and Santa Claus and becomes obsessed with the idea that if he replaces Santa Claus, he'll get the satisfaction and fulfilment that he longs for. He is then motivated to go and achieve that goal.

Whilst he's expressing his longing for another life, he's being followed around by Sally who is in love with him, but he doesn't know. It's a visual clue for the fact that during the course of the film he learns that what he's longing for isn't actually a different life, it's to be in love.

As you follow Jack Skellington, you watch him following the lie he believes to be true. The fact it's a lie is what gets in the way of his happiness, until he accepts the truth, and goes home to be with Sally. The audience is discovering the truth as Jack Skellington does, and that's what you can take into your own writing.

Your Audience is Connected to your Protagonist

When using this device in your own writing, you keep to your Protagonist's point of view, so the story presents as if what the Protagonist believes is true. Together your audience and your Protagonist discover the truth, and that keeps your audience and the Protagonist connected. Your audience is going on the journey with them, and even if on an emotional level they realise that it's a lie, everybody has to discover the truth together.

Your audience can learn the truth a little bit before your Protagonist. Not a long time before as they need to be rooted to your Protagonist's experiences, and if it's too obvious too soon they'll feel disconnected. But if they realise it just a bit before, they can then watch the story unfold in a satisfying way as the Protagonist discovers the truth, excited to witness that realisation.

This is something you can play with. Make sure you reveal it to your audience in a subtle and effective way by planting seeds throughout the story that hint towards it, without revealing it to your Protagonist.

A Layer of Conflict

This is a really useful writing technique to make your Protagonist's story arc interesting and keep your audience invested in them and connected to them.

Giving your Protagonist something they want and sending them in pursuit of it is always the first step in story creation and making that thing a lie is an interesting device that just makes it more layered with conflict and, therefore, more interesting.

XXIV
From the Mundane to the Magical

Taking your characters from the mundane to the magical is a technique used in most fantasy stories. It is the process of taking your character from their normal life in their ordinary world that they're familiar with, and into a magical world that's new. I'll be exploring that transition, explaining how to use it for your story.

The Lion, the Witch and the Wardrobe

The C. S. Lewis book *The Lion, the Witch and the Wardrobe* is a perfect example of this transition between the mundane and the magical being used. The wardrobe is a literal door that the characters pass through to leave the mundane world and enter the magical one.

At the start of the story, Susan, Lucy, Peter and Edward are living in the big old house in the English countryside, when they discover the magical wardrobe. When they enter the wardrobe, they transition from that mundane world, and into the magical world of Narnia.

Transitioning to a Different World

The journey from the mundane to the magical can be represented in many different ways. In *Alice In Wonderland*, Lewis Carroll used a rabbit hole. In the *Harry Potter* series, J. K. Rowling used the train to Hogwarts. But there is a step that must be taken to leave the familiar world the characters live in and enter this new world that they will explore.

It's important to remember that the mundane world you start in is mundane to the character, not the audience. For instance, in *Star Wars: Episode IV – A New Hope*, Luke Skywalker starts on his home planet of Tatooine, which seems fantastical to the audience because it's an alien planet, but it's his version of Earth. He then journeys into the magical when he goes into space and learns to use "The Force".

Your story will then follow your character on their journey through the magical world, where their adventures happen. Because both the characters and the audience are outsiders to that magical world, the audience will discover the rules of that world alongside them. Be it The Force, or magic, or strange creatures etc, you learn at the same time and thus the audience and the characters are connected by that discovery.

Crossing A Barrier

The mundane to the magical is a really beautiful device to use because doorways are a metaphor for transition, which is why *The Lion, the Witch and the Wardrobe* is such a perfect example because of the literal use of a door.

The barrier is there, it prevents you reaching the magical world, then when you open the door you cross that threshold. Opening the door can come in many forms, such as Neo taking the red pill in *The Matrix* which opens his metaphorical door by opening his mind to reality.

Yearning for More

The character you take from the mundane to the magical should have a yearning for more. If they don't dream of adventure or discovery, they won't be motivated to take the step to cross that barrier. Whatever it is they want they need to hope the answer is found on the other side of that door.

XXV
Time-Locks

A "time-lock" is best to use in your story when you've established who your Protagonist and Antagonist are. You've pitted them against each other, but your story lacks pressure and haste. You want to ramp up the tension and manipulate the circumstances surrounding your characters, so the story is more exciting. A time-lock gives your story energy, and is what tells your audience and your characters, that you're headed for the climax.

Sports movies are a really good place to find examples of a time-lock in story. The big final match is looming at the end of the story, so everything the characters do is with an awareness that that game will be the climax. Think of Rocky's big final fight, the big game at the end of *Dodgeball*, and the last stage of the cheerleading competition in *Bring It On*.

Examples of Time-Locks

If you're writing a book or film that doesn't have a built in time-lock, you can add it to your story by forcing your characters into a situation where they have to get something completed by a certain time.

For instance, in *Lilly Prospero and the Magic Rabbit*, I wrote a time-lock. With as few spoilers as possible, Lilly is studying at a special facility and hears about a "Final Gathering". She then has to work out if that is a good thing or a bad thing, who she can trust and work with, and how to control her magical power before it happens. It adds pressure on the character and builds towards the climax with an energy that might not otherwise be there.

Another excellent example you can watch and learn from is from season five of *Buffy the Vampire Slayer*. The Big Bad is Glory, a God from a Hell dimension who comes to Earth and needs to find a mystical key that will bleed the Hell dimension into ours.

Buffy and her friends find out there is a specific time and place where Glory can do this spell, and use the key, and that puts pressure on them to stop her quickly, and on Glory to find the key in time to do the spell in time. As time gets closer, it ramps up the tension and drama of the story, which is excellent for the audience to witness.

How to Add a Time-Lock

When you're writing your story, if you feel like you need to add tension and drama and escalation to your story, a time-lock is a perfect way of doing it. It is both more entertaining and easier to steer your story towards the climax when the tension is ramping up.

The time-lock could be something as dramatic as Hell bleeding onto Earth, or as simple as an opportunity coming up that won't last forever. But the application of this time-lock factor increases motivation, and immediately raises the stakes, for everybody involved immediately.

The time-lock is best introduced as a mid-point turning point, or at the end of act two as you charge towards the climax. A sports or competition movie tends to have the time-lock in place from the very beginning, but usually it would be added later as another layer of pressure after the story is already underway.

Ultimately, think of your time-lock as your Protagonist finding out that if they don't succeed now, they can never succeed, and dealing with those consequences.

XXVI
The "Death of the Mentor"

The "Death of the Mentor" is a technique used in storytelling to motivate the Protagonist, by killing the person who has taught them to do what it is they do. It's a well-used trope, and thus must be used with awareness and caution to avoid predictability, but it can still work really well. I'll talk you through what it means, what it does for your story, and how you can make it work in your own writing.

Obi Wan Kenobi

The classic example of the death of a mentor being written for this purpose is the death of Obi Wan Kenobi in *Star Wars: Episode IV - A New Hope*.

Luke Skywalker meets Obi Wan Kenobi who teaches him what The Force is and how to use it, about his family, etc., and then gets killed by Darth Vader, which motivates Luke to do better throughout the rest of the film. Prior to the death of Obi Wan, Luke was unable to complete is story journey. Forcing Luke to stand alone without the support makes him stronger.

It's probably to blame for the trope becoming cliched because of how effective it was at the time, but it's also a really good demonstration of how and why it is used.

Parody

The frequency of use, and fame of this trope, makes it easily parodied. In *The Office*, Michael Scott's movie, *Threat Level Midnight*, features the death of a mentor in a perfectly done parody.

Cherokee Jack, played by Creed Bratton (played by Creed Bratton), is Michael Scarn's ice hockey mentor. He is killed by the antagonist, Goldenface, three quarters of the way into the film. This then propels Michael Scarn towards the climax with purpose, forced to stand alone without his help.

The reason the death of this character is such a perfect parody is because as well as being a perfectly executed joke, it's also a really clear and well-constructed example of how to write it in your own story. When Cherokee Jack dies, it motivates Michael Scarn perfectly to accomplish his goals in a way he previously felt unable to.

I would genuinely recommend seeking it out and watching it just to see how well structured it is and how the death of the mentor is used, whilst acknowledging it is a clear parody and very funny with it.

Where Do You Use It?

If you're writing in a three-act structure, the death of the mentor is best placed at the end of the second act. It will then send your Protagonist on their path to accomplish what it is they want to accomplish in Act 3, in a way they didn't feel able to do prior to their mentor's death.

Even if what they set out to do ends in defeat, they were not previously motivated sufficiently or feeling capable of even trying until this happens.

How to Write "The Death of the Mentor"

Being such a well-known trope can make using it something of an issue. Your audience is likely to see it coming and therefore it will have probably less impact, unless you can really make them feel.

To make the most effective death of a mentor, aim to cause the absolute maximum pain you can. This will stop your audience thinking about the cliché, because they'll be too busy feeling their emotions.

I have written the death of a mentor in my own writing (*Lilly Prospero and the Magic Rabbit*), and I made the choice to deal with the cliché by causing the reader as much emotional devastation as possible. It draws the focus away from the predictability because your reader is too busy coping with their pain.

It sounds evil, but it's effective, and allows you to have the impact of it in your story without it being ruined.

Another method you could use to get over the cliché factor is, instead of a literal death, have the mentor be lost to your Protagonist in some other way. They could be taken away emotionally, so your Protagonist now feels alone.

Why Does "Death of the Mentor" Work?

The mentor character is very common in fantasy stories, because your Protagonist needs a guide to explain the magical world they're now in and teach them about the powers or magic of that world. When that mentor is taken away, it then forces your character to stand on their own two feet in this new world they're adapting to.

In whatever way your mentor is lost to your Protagonist, losing that support and that guidance is what gives them enough motivation to finally take the final steps they need. It could be to avenge their death or prove them wrong, or it could be to live up to the faith the mentor had in them to honour their memory.

But either way, that loss takes your Protagonist through the transition from unable to go for their final goal, into willing to do it. You just need to be aware that you're treading footsteps previously trodden and it's very easy to slip into predictable cliché if you don't handle it with care.

XXVII
Coincidences

A coincidence in a story is an event that has no foreshadowing and your character didn't directly cause. It isn't something the character looked for and it isn't the consequence of previous action. The coincidence just happens to them and impacts them, and then they react to it

Coincidences can trigger a story, or progress an existing story, but they have to be handled with care. Having too many coincidences in your story can make it weak, and it shows a lack of planning and intent. I'll be writing about why coincidences are a problem, and how to avoid writing them.

The Problem with Coincidences

When you're telling your story, you're trying to emulate life to a certain extent, and because coincidences do happen in life, you can usually get away with using one coincidence in your story.

If something strikingly coincidental and unusual happens in your story, say a character wins the lottery, you'll find that your audience can go with you. But if you start layering these coincidences then they won't. It becomes unbelievable and, somewhat, pointless.

That's not a story, that's just a series of chance events that a character is reacting to. Even if *technically* you could have a long series of life changing coincidences happening, because life is random and coincidences are a possibility, it doesn't make for a good story.

Solving a Problem with a Fluke

When your character goes to find the information and accomplishes that goal, you have a good story. When they chance upon it by coincidence, you have a fluke. And it happens quite regularly in stories that the Protagonist bumps into somebody who happens to have the information they need, or they happen to be in the same diner as criminals discussing their plans.

The accidental information discovery means your character hasn't struggled, overcome a challenge, and hasn't learned anything or developed as a person. What they need has just landed in their lap.

When the information that solves a problem for them that they've been struggling with throughout your entire story comes to them by chance, it feels unearned. It's never believable, it's always a bit of an eyeroll, and it's completely avoidable.

When you're writing your character attempting to overcome a problem, you're essentially trying to figure out overcome that problem yourself. And if you can't figure out how to, writing them chancing upon it is just your way of getting out of that problem easily for yourself, rather than putting the effort in and figuring out what to do. And that comes across. It's boring and lazy storytelling.

Make Your Character Work for It

You can write a character getting information in the exact same way as they would by accident, but make it entertaining and story-worthy. Say you want them to overhear people talking in a diner, and originally you wrote it by chance. Go back into your story and make them earn that information. Write them working out *where* the person who has the information will be to talk about it, write them making the plan to be at the same diner at the same time, with the purpose of overhearing it.

If your criminals are gathering in a diner to talk, your police officer would either tail one of them, worth reading or watching.

Seeing characters struggle and push and overcome conflict in their path to accomplish their goals is entertaining. Watching them learn and improve in their competency as their character arc moves forward is entertaining. The struggle is the point of the story. The sense at the end of a story when things have just fallen into place by coincidence, rather than your character pushing them into place, is of disappointment, not satisfaction.

When Can You Use a Coincidence?

If you choose to have a coincidence in your tale, it shouldn't be the key to solving the entire story. It is better suited to launching your story than solving it, and if it is too big and significant an event being done by coincidence, it becomes boring and unbelievable.

Significant information and key events need to be written with intent, and a coincidence feels lazy and inept.

If you want to tell a story where a series of striking events happen, and in theory they could be coincidences, then you need to pick one to be a coincidence. Everything after that needs to be as a result of direct action taken by your characters in response to that initial coincidence.

What to Write Instead of a Coincidence

When you have simple scenario to write, such as two characters bumping into each other in the supermarket, it is tempting to make it a coincidence. It's not a key event and just helps your plot tick forwards. However, you can still avoid making it feel like a coincidence to your audience by using foreshadowing.

If earlier in the story you mention that one character is going to a party and needs to buy supplies, and the other character is going to make dinner and needs ingredients, you have then reason for them to be in the same place at the same time. It will feel natural and real, without needing to shine a light on it as it happens.

Foreshadowing is how you can build to any event without having to use a coincidence. Narrative Triplets are the perfect way of foreshadowing any event into feeling like it was planned and constructed.

Sew into your story two previous mentions or incidences of your later coincidence, and by the time that third time comes around your audience will feel like it was intended from the start. Something planned like this is much more satisfying.

It can still be a surprise, with subtle foreshadowing, but it won't feel like an unbelievable coincidence.

Make Your Characters Work

How to Write a Story

If when you get to the end of your story, and there's a final obstacle your character has to overcome, it might be tempting to let that be easy for them by way of a coincidence because of how much they've already been through. It's often referred to as "deus ex machina" which means that a problem is suddenly fixed by an act of God. A simple coincidence that ties a final bow on your story for your character.

But resist that, make it a challenge, make that final obstacle something your character has to work for and overcome at cost and pain to themselves. A coincidence at the end of your story feels too easy and your audience will feel deflated and unsatisfied.

Coincidences imply you can't be bothered, or you're not capable, of writing a complete and well-constructed story. Put the time and effort in, because your story and your audience are worth it.

If when you're writing your story you find you have written yourself into a situation where you cannot think how to get your character the information they need without a coincidence, take a break. Walk away from it and let yourself think, because if you put the effort in to make it consequences of your character's actions not just happenstance, it'll be worth it.

XXVIII
How to Write Suspense

If you are writing a scary story, or a thriller or a mystery, suspense is one of the key things you need to make your story appealing to your audience. It will keep them excited and intrigued so they will want to stay with you and keep watching or reading to the end. I'll be explaining the technique to use to build suspense in your story, and referencing *13 Reasons Why,* season three.

Questions Build Suspense

The best way to build suspense is to give your characters, and your audience, questions about your story that you then delay answering. Slowly, through your story, your audience and your characters, will start to learn the truth as you drip feed the answers they want.

When you're posing these questions, such as who killed someone and why, you have to make sure you live up to the promise you make to answer most of them.

Leaving *some* unanswered questions is fine—things that leave your audience pondering when the story has finished—but most should be answered. Answering them slowly and strategically is key to suspense. Not answering them at all is the key to being irritating.

Whodunit

If you look at a mystery story as an example, you'll likely have one central question: your "whodunit" question. Who, or what, is responsible for this murder? It won't necessarily be a murder in the centre of your story, but I'll use that as an example here.

That "whodunit" question will be what occupies the mind of your Protagonist so much that they change their behaviour and set about finding the answer through the course of your story.

From the initial "whodunit" question, you then spread out to more questions that dominate your story:

Who killed the guy?
Why did he kill the guy?
What did he use to kill the guy?
Where did he kill the guy?
Who was the guy connected to?
Who witnessed the guy being killed?

These questions can spread and spread out from that central "whodunit" question that your story pivots on, and through the story you slowly reveal the answers, building up the tension and pressure to find out more answers. As you reveal certain answers, more questions can spring up. Keep the questions coming and make your audience desperate for the answers.

13 Reasons Why

An excellent example of this slow question answering to build suspense around a murder is in *13 Reasons Why*, season three. If you've not seen it, this next section will contain spoilers.

The season surrounds the central question of who killed Bryce. Slowly through the story you start to learn details, such as that he was murdered and other people were on the scene, which give you more questions. These questions build up, you learn that some characters have answers to some of the questions, whilst others know the answers to others.

As the story moves forward, you learn some of these answers, you're ahead of some characters and behind others and you keep asking more. All these questions pivot around the central "whodunit" question.

The suspense is built throughout this season until you reach the final episode, because slowly you're learning answers as the pressure builds so you're constantly waiting and eager for more, and desperate for the final answer. Who killed Bryce?

One Central Question

Placing one central question to hang your story off, then surrounding that question by a spiderweb of other questions to answer as the story moves forward, is how to build up your story suspense.

Making sure you answer these questions, slowly but surely, is one difference between suspense and confusion. You want your audience to be desperate for answers because they're intrigued, not because they're confused.

So, remember, ask a big central question, pose several other questions around that central question that you slowly answer through the story, so your audience gets more and more desperate for the final big answer, and that is how you'll write suspense.

XXIX
Making the Unbelievable Believable

If you are writing in the fantasy, urban fantasy, paranormal, or sci-fi genres, you're going to be writing scenarios for your characters that are, technically, unbelievable. In reality, people don't believe that the White House is going to be blown up by aliens or that witches and wizards are being trained in magic in a big school, yet we are able to believe it in the story because of how it's written.

Characters Build Believability

The way to make your unbelievable stories feel real, is by having your characters react in a real way. As long as your characters behave in a way that feels realistic, the most unbelievable story will still work. Where this often goes wrong, is when a character is suddenly an expert in something for no reason.

For instance, if you write aliens landing and your Protagonist is suddenly an expert in alien language, with no foreshadowing, no evidence in their past that would explain it, that would be unbelievable. The fact that aliens landing is quite unbelievable doesn't matter, it's how your character reacts to it that will boot your audience out.

Another temptation you might have is to change your character's personality on a pin, just because it suits your story in that moment. So, aliens have landed, but this time the most underconfident and shy character you have is in the best position to go and try to communicate with them, so you write that they do it. Again, your audience will go with you on the aliens landing, but you'll lose them if your character behaves incorrectly.

Focus on How Your Characters React

For any circumstances you write, no matter how unbelievable and unrelatable they seem, put a lot of focus and energy into making sure your characters respond to it in a way that *is* believable and relatable.

No matter how extraordinary the situation you're writing is, your audience can believe in it. However, as soon as your audience stops reading or watching to think about how nobody would do that, nobody would say that, or wonder how come a character can suddenly do something they couldn't do before, you've lost them.

Characters Are Genre Aware

Another thing to consider is, your characters will be genre aware. If they live in our world, you cannot introduce characters to vampires, ghosts, werewolves, zombies etc., and have them unaware of what those things are. You have to reflect that in how they behave towards whatever supernatural story element you've introduced.

A really good example of this being done well is in *Shaun of the Dead*. When zombies are introduced to the story, they acknowledge how crazy it is.

Having characters reference pop culture examples of whatever it is they're dealing with is a really good way of connecting those characters to your audience. If you're writing for people who came of age in the noughties, and vampires or werewolves are introduced to the story, then it would be believable to your audience that some of those characters would reference *Buffy the Vampire Slayer* or *Twilight*.

Foreshadowing

The way to get around needing to have characters with the knowledge or skills they need for the story or have a personality arc that makes them behave in a way the story situation requires, is to foreshadow. *Always* foreshadow.

For instance, in *The Lost World: Jurassic Park*, when Dr. Ian Malcolm's daughter Kelly does the impressive gymnast flip that boots a velociraptor out of a window and saves the day, it's been mentioned previously about how talented she is at gymnastics. Had the previous mentions of her gymnastic training not been done, the audience would have been immediately booted from the story as the ability would seem nonsensical. As it is, it's far-fetched and ludicrous as an idea, but it still works for the story.

If you write yourself into a situation where you need a character to do amazing gymnastics to save your other characters from a velociraptor, don't let the fact that the scenario is ridiculous stop you. In and of itself, the situation is unbelievable, but if you foreshadow it correctly and make sure your characters all respond to it in a believable way, your story won't come across as unbelievable.

Edit Well

Anything you write into your story that feels like it has come out of nowhere, but needed to happen in the moment, can be fixed.

By editing your story, you can make any scenario seem real by carefully controlling your characters. If you need a character to be able to boot a velociraptor in the face, go back into your story and find a reason why a character's ability at gymnastics is either mentioned or demonstrated in the earlier part of your story, at least once but preferably twice, for a completely different reason.

Always remember, any unbelievable story concept will work, as long as your characters behave in a believable way.

XXX
Your Character's Arc

When you first introduce your characters, they will have a certain personality type and behaviours. Through the course of your story, your characters will grow and change due to their experiences, and have emotional responses to the environment they're in. This is known as your character's arc.

I'll be explaining what your character's arc does for your story, the impact of failing to track it consistently, and how to make your character's arc work for your story.

Character's Emotions

It's always important to make sure your character's emotions are appropriate to the scene they're in, so if the scene is scary, make sure your character is scared, if the scene is heart-breaking, make sure they're sad. But then those emotions need to have impact beyond just the initial scene.

Tracking your character's emotional state is an essential part of continuity when it comes to your character's arc. When your character experiences emotions, you need to make sure you carry the ramifications of that with them into the subsequent scenes. Characters emotions need to move with the story, rather than just being set back to neutral.

When Emotions Aren't Tracked

An example of a character's emotional state not being tracked, and the negative impact that then has on the story, is from *Lost*, season one, "The Moth". During this episode, Charlie, who is struggling with drug addiction, makes the choice to get rid of his supply of heroin. Of course, this leads Charlie to go through heroin withdrawal; he's emotional and sweating and shaking.

The next episode, "Confidence Man," starts the following morning and Charlie is completely fine. He's focused on getting peanut butter for Claire and not showing signs of the distress he was in just hours earlier. His emotional state has not been carried with him.

The impact of failing to track your characters emotional state in this way is that the character feels inconsistent and the audience is emotionally disconnected from them. You need to show the journey from one emotional state into another or the character is broken to suit the story, rather than moving through the story as part of it.

Arcing Your Characters

The art of tracking character's emotional states successfully is known as arcing your character. If you want to take your character from one emotional state to another, even if those emotions are completely at odds with one another, you absolutely can.

Showing the process, the arc, is the only way to do it well. You can take your character from happy to sad, weak to strong, etc, as long as you take the audience on that journey with them.

The problem you will face as a writer is that carrying all these emotional states in your head at all times can be draining. If you're moving between different characters and different scenes, and there's quite a break between them, it can be hard to track them. And it gets a larger weight to carry the further into a series you get, because you're carrying historical emotions that will bump and flare up through the course of the story.

How to Do It

The best way to do it successfully is to find a way to chart your characters. I keep a spreadsheet of every character I have ever written in every book or script. I include anything that has happened to them of significance, any emotional bonds they have with other characters, anything they're scared of, and anything they're passionate about. This is then something I can refer back to at any point when I'm writing or during the editing process to make sure they're consistent and reacting to any given scenario I've put them in as they should.

I've been writing some of these characters for years, my *Lilly Prospero* series for instance, and a lot happens to them during that time. I'm also writing a number of other characters in TV and film scripts, as well as other books. With that many people in my head, I can easily lose track of all those lives and emotions over the course of that time.

Spreadsheets like this might seem like a crazy obsessive thing to do, but for me it makes sure I feel confident that I'm doing the best job I can. Because that's exactly what this is—my job, and I treat it as such. I don't want to break my characters, and this is how I guard against it.

Spreadsheets aren't for everyone, and some people will feel in control of managing these emotional states for everybody they create in their head. If you can do that, I'm in awe, because I really can't. If you can't manage that, like me, I highly recommend finding a way of tracking your characters emotional states that works for you.

Foreshadowing

If you're writing a story where you want a character to do something dramatic for the sake of the plot, such as kill somebody, you need to foreshadow that as a possibility for them. If you don't foreshadow it, you're making your character behave in a way that is atypical to how you've previously established that person to be, which will throw your audience out.

They don't need to like your character, but they need to believe your character will do what you make them do.

If you want to send your character on a journey towards killing, you can do it with absolutely any character. Even the most innocent and gentle character can be pushed into circumstances where they would kill, and if you want to show a character was supressing or hiding a desire to kill you can do that too with their behaviour. But it has to be foreshadowed. You have to let your audience in on the experience your character is having.

How to Make it Believable

In TV shows you often find they need a romantic relationship for drama and conflict, so they decide to throw two characters together. You might get a couple of episodes where they start checking each other out, and then bam, they've shoved them together. It alienates audiences when it doesn't need to.

If you build up more slowly, show them interacting and making one another feel good, show them having tension between them build up, you'll find audiences much more willing to go with a love interest, no matter how abstract it might seem at first.

Secondary Characters Need the Same Care

Sometimes you'll find that you will be careful with your Protagonist and Antagonist, your main characters, because you might have put a lot of time and energy into planning their personality. You know who they are and they're consistent and moving through the story as solid people in your mind.

Your character breaks will happen with people circulating around them, your secondary characters, who you create as devices to help move the story along and for your Protagonist and Antagonist to interact with. Because your secondary characters are less important, you might have them behave in ways that are just convenient, perhaps pick a fight with your Protagonist for scene-level drama, or flirt with your Protagonist's love interest.

Again, any of these scenarios are fine as long as you treat each character like the Protagonist in their own story and ensure any behaviour is either consistent with the character from the beginning or arced to with experiences or foreshadowing.

Building to a Plot Twist

The build to a plot twist or development, such as a murder or a relationship, via foreshadowing or the gradual change as pressure builds or tension grows between characters, is known as arcing. You're taking your audience with you on that curve between one emotional or mental state to another and showing your audience why your character is behaving in a certain way.

With a well-constructed character arc, you'll have your audience accepting even the most extreme circumstances you decide to put your characters in. Breaking your characters will lose your audience because if they don't believe in your characters, they won't believe in your story.

XXXI
Exploring the Point of View Character Concept

When you're constructing a novel, usually you write in the first or third person. "First person" refers to the Protagonist as I, and "third person" refers to the Protagonist as He or She. Building on the previous chapter, I'm going to be explaining the use of a point of view character in third person, and how you can use them for connecting your reader to the other characters in the scene and the setting they're in, without overloading your audience with unnecessary detail.

The Point of View Character

When you're writing a scene, you should try to remain in one character's point of view. For most scenes this will be your Protagonist, your main character, but you'll write scenes that don't have the Protagonist in them, or you might want to hop to someone else's point of view to demonstrate how other people are interpreting your Protagonist's behaviour. But when you start a scene in one character's point of view, you should stay in that person's point of view until either the end of the scene, by moving to a new setting, or until you break the scene with a scene break but stay in the same place.

You don't usually need to announce whose point of view you're in, even though you're referring to the character's by name rather than "I" because it's apparent whose point of view it is by the information you give about the scene, and that information is what I'm going to be explaining.

Show Don't Tell

Your point of view character is how you paint the picture of the scene to your audience by filling in the spaces between the dialogue to create the scene in their head.

For instance, if your point of view character walks into a room, they will have feelings about that room. It might be connected to their emotional response to the other people in that room, and you can describe pertinent information about the other characters and where they are, how they're standing and any known history on them, by the way your point of view character feels. Their feelings might be connected to the room itself, any smells that trigger a response, any memories the room has connected to it.

When another character speaks, you can describe their tone, their body language, their expressions because that will impact how your point of view character feels about what they're saying. You don't have to let the audience know if they're lying, but you can let your audience know that your point of view character is suspicious of them and why. You don't tell your audience if the other character is sad, but you can have your point of view character notice a tear in their eye or a crack in their voice.

As the narrator you're not God, you don't have access to every single thought and feeling in the room, but you can still give your audience enough information that they can understand the other characters in the scene, but without overloading them.

Setting the Scene

The impact of filling in the details of the scene in this way is grounding the details of your story in humanity. Your audience come to your story for the characters; what they want, how they're going about getting it, and what obstacles they have to face.

Setting the scene should enhance that story, rather than distracting from it. If you take so much time describing the environment your characters are in so clearly that your audience can picture them perfectly, you risk taking so much time away from the story that your readers don't care anymore.

Your audience will be infinitely more interested in your scene if the information they get about it relates directly to the point of view character. The colour of the chairs in the room isn't interesting, but how your character feels about the people sitting in the chairs is. The placement of the chairs in isolation isn't interesting, but what it means for where your character has to sit and how they feel about it is. Describing the paintings on the wall isn't interesting, but if they remind your character of home or give them the creeps, it is.

When you write a film script, all these extra details are filled in by costume and set designers, the way actors deliver lines, and the composer setting the mood. For a book it's your job to do it, and to do it in enough details that your readers understand the scene they're in, are interested in it, and feel emotionally connected to it.

By rooting in one point of view character, and only describing the things in the scene that directly affect them, and which they're interested in, you don't overload your writing with so much description that your audience is bored.

Focusing on Humanity

Grounding your descriptions in the humanity of your point of view character and keeping them relevant to their immediate feelings, makes your descriptions interesting, and keeps your audience invested. We go to stories for humanity, for characters and their story, so keep your whole story connected to that.

XXXII
Making Characters' Motivations Understandable

I've written about how your Protagonist and your Antagonist both have to be motivated to go after what it is that they want, but it's important to remember that your audience has to understand why they want it. If they don't understand why it matters, disconnect from the character and stop caring if they achieve their goals.

When Motivation Doesn't Make Sense

In *Game of Thrones*, throughout the series, Daenerys is demonstrated to be motivated to reclaim the Iron Throne, and to be a powerful leader. She considers herself worthy of loyalty and worship, and a true Queen. This is until suddenly Jon Snow seems to change her, and she starts expressing a desire to be worthy of him. She becomes motivated to prove herself to him, rather than expecting him to prove himself to her.

There has been no build up to this change, there seems to be no reason for this desire to be impressive, as she's always considered herself impressive anyway. For the audience, there is a massive disconnect. We know she wants it; we know it matters to her, but we've been left out of the reason why it matters so it feels unnatural and we can't fully believe in it.

Inexplicable motivations are a frequent problem with Antagonists. You know they want to do something dastardly, such as destroy the world, but you don't know why. Especially considering they live on it too.

Being active in pursuit of their goals is good, and what I will constantly tell you to do. But why it matters to them is just as important as having it matter in the first place. Inexplicable motivation is confusing and off-putting.

Demonstrate Frustration

A simple way to demonstrate why something motivates a character is to show their frustrations. Something about their life and circumstances is frustrating them enough that they become motivated to change it. You can make any character's motivations understandable if you can demonstrate how it came to matter to them. This can be achieved by showing them prior to taking action, the inciting incident being the moment they move from passive to active, or you can show it through flashbacks, or with conversations about it in their present circumstances.

As long as you take the time and care to make sure it's clear why something matters to your character, you can make almost any action feel understandably motivated.

By grounding your audience in what motivates your characters, so even if they wouldn't do something themselves or they actively disagree with the choice being made, they can at least feel connected to that character enough to understand why they're doing something. Nobody feels like they're acting randomly or just for the sake of moving your story forward without any thought put in as to why.

Different Kinds of Villain

The exception to the rule is when you come to villains who are designed to be horrifying or shocking. For instance, Joker in *The Dark Knight* is doing all kinds of things that he's clearly very motivated to do, but you're not given a reason that is understandable or relatable to most people. He's an agent of chaos, and chaos and destruction are motivation enough.

If your character is a truly evil person who hurts people in brutal ways, if you demonstrate how they got to that point and explain their motivation, it can humanise them in a way that stops them being frightening.

However, in *Spider-Man: Into the Spider-Verse*, the villainous Kingpin is a dangerous man who is motivated to do terrible and destructive things, but one of the reasons the character is so interesting and captivating is because the root cause for that motivation is understandable; he misses his family and is grieving.

Having a base for the motivation that you understand and relate to, before he goes to extremes, means the audience can connect to the character more than if he seemed to just be doing something evil so that Spider-Man has a bad guy to fight.

Grounding Your Audience in Your Character

Giving your character something to pursue, and a reason for that pursuit, is a solid grounding for a good story. If your characters feel like they're only doing something because you as the writer feel like writing about it, and there's no other reason for them to behave in that way, your characters stop feeling real and your audience will stop caring.

XXXIII
How to Make Your Audience Cry

If you are writing something absolutely devastating in your story, such as a heartbreak or a death scene, it's natural as a writer that you want to make your audience cry when it happens. If they cry, that means you have successfully connected with them in a way that is powerful enough to move them, which means your story is well written enough to connect with.

There are two ways you can go about reeking emotional devastation on your audience.

Piling On Tragedy

The first way is by writing something that is just really terribly sad and hoping that you push a button enough that it has an impact on your reader.

So, you write that your character leaves his dog in the house for the day, and then the house burns down, killing the dog. That is a devastatingly sad incident in any story and would definitely move some people to tears. However, if your audience doesn't know your character or his dog, doesn't know why the dog matters so much to him, and hasn't spent any time with them enough to know how much losing the dog would mean to him, most people won't be particularly upset by the scene.

Writing terribly sad things that, in and of themselves, are very upsetting, is not enough. That's just trying to make people cry but without any care or any heart put into the work. It's cold. Cold sadness doesn't stick with people and it doesn't move people, it's just acknowledged as sad and then you move on with the story.

Emotionally Connect to Your Audience

To make the same scene an emotional bullet, you take the time to tell your audience about the character and his dog. Build the relationship, develop the connection and show why the dog matters so much. Have scenes with your character depending on the dog for comfort and company, show their bond growing and how much the dog loves him. Then, when he leaves the dog in the house, show that he has prioritised something over the dog that he shouldn't have, show the dog sad that he's being left behind.

Then burn the dog.

If you want to go even further for more emotional pain, after tragedy throw in hope. So, before the dog died, he'd had a relationship with a lady dog and then she births a litter of puppies and your character can take one home and begin the journey again, with a new dog.

It's brutal and calculated, but that's the job. If you want to make people cry, you have to put time and energy into making them connect with the characters that you're going to break their hearts with. To make them connect to the character, you have to give them reasons to care, so layer reasons why that character or that relationship matter, then give them hopes and dreams for that character that you never realise.

If it's a couple you're going to break up, make your audience hope for their wedding or their child. If you're going to kill someone, make your audience want something for them that they can never have.

Stories That Make Me Cry

Stories that have made me break my heart and ugly-cry, such as *Charlotte's Web*, *Watership Down*, *Tinker Bell and the Legend of the NeverBeast*, and *The Notebook*, have had that impact on me because by the time you get to moving moment, I'm already invested in the characters and care about them deeply.

When the old couple lie down together at the end of *The Notebook*, cuddle up and die, I am a broken woman. I cannot breathe I'm crying so hard. If you'd shown me that old couple at the beginning of the film, I'd have thought it was very sad and moving, but I wouldn't have been broken because they're not my people. By the end of the film they're my people, I care, I'm invested in them, so their deaths have an emotional impact on me.

Making Your Audience Care Makes Them Cry

If you just want to make people cry but can't be bothered to invest time into connecting with your audience, you can throw tragedy after tragedy into your story and maybe poke enough bruises in your audience that you make them cry. But it won't be real, it won't stick, and they won't carry that emotion with them after your story finishes.

If you want to make people cry because they care about your characters and will carry your story in your heart for years after they've read it, you have to treat both your audience and your story with the respect of investing in them.

Build to the sadness, grow the audience's bond with your story, demonstrate why the characters matter and give the audience something to hope for. If they want good things for that character, and their lives matter to them, then you shatter that hope, you'll have the exact right amount of emotional devastation.

XXXIV
Launching a Series with a Cliffhanger

If you are planning a series of books or films, then you need to write the first one in a way that will encourage your audience to come back for the second instalment and excite them to read further adventures with those characters. One way of doing that is with a cliffhanger, so you leave part of your story untold and end it at a point of tension that the audience hopes to be resolved next time. However, there are negative consequences to that decision.

No Guarantee You'll Resolve the Conflict

When you buy a book or film, you're spending money, and investing time, to experience a story. Ending the first instalment of a series on a cliffhanger is placing a massive assumption on your audience that they'll be willing to return, especially when you haven't yet demonstrated you're able to tell a complete story and charged them to get part of a story without their consent.

Your main story is following a conflict. Your Protagonist wants something, and they're going after it whilst things get in their way, and your story ends when that conflict is resolved, and they either have what they want, or they don't.

If you choose to end this portion of your story before that conflict is resolved, you're giving no guarantee to your audience that you are able to resolve it, nor any time scale of when it will be resolved. Without a guarantee of when your story will end, your audience won't know how much more money and time will be required from them to get satisfaction.

What to Do Instead of Writing a Cliffhanger

If you want to tee up a sequel by leaving conflict unresolved, you can do it as long as it's with small threads, not with the main plot.

Small plotlines that are left unresolved with the promise of more to come can make your reader excited that you have plans to grow and expand in that world, without leaving them unsatisfied and frustrated that they signed up for a story and only got a piece of one.

For instance, if you look at *Harry Potter and the Philosopher's Stone*, that book launches a successful series. The conflict you're signed up for is about the philosopher's stone; what it does, who wants it, and who will get it. That conflict is resolved at the end and the story is complete. However, the threads are left open to entice you back for more, because you're told Voldemort will want to come back.

If no more books were ever written, you've still experienced a complete story, but it's drawing you in to read on to find out if he'll come back and what happens when he does. If she'd ended the book before Harry had faced Quirrell and Voldemort, then the first book would have been far less enjoyable, and nobody would have known if it was worth coming back for more.

Mistakes I Made

When I first started writing I had a lot to learn, which is why I was writing for years before a book came out. And this specific lesson is one I had to be taught.

When I started writing *Lilly Prospero and the Magic Rabbit*, my first book, I tried ending it on a cliffhanger. The entire book built up to what is now my midpoint, because I felt like it was a dramatic and exciting moment and would make people want to read more. But I hadn't written more.

I started the book with Lilly's conflict, which is that she has the power to create life and she doesn't know how to use it nor what the consequences are, and ended it with a striking development, but not a resolution. Obviously, now it's resolved at the end. However, the world is now different for Lilly and there was plenty of space for that story to grow into, without being an unsatisfying ending.

New Audiences Have to Be Treated with Care

With a first book you have no guarantee that there will be a sequel. No guarantee of how long it will be until that sequel is released. There's no way of knowing if and when a conflict will be resolved if you leave it hanging, and your audience will all be left unsatisfied, which is not the overwhelming feeling you want from your readers if you expect them to come back for more. A first book is delicate, and has to be treated as such, because it could launch your world, or it could turn everybody off and destroy it.

When you're further along and have a solid audience base and can afford to be more experimental and play around with your stories, then you can try a cliffhanger end if it appeals to you, because you know they'll come back for more because of how much they've already invested in your world and your characters. But until you've earned that loyalty, it's foolish to test it.

XXXV
Writing Enemies to Friends

Characters that start out as enemies, and through the course of the story turn into friends or lovers is quite a popular trope, and because it's popular it's used a lot. It can work really well, and satisfy your audience in a specific way, or it can just feel predictable and dull, depending on how you use it. I'll explain why it is popular, and how you can make it work in your own story.

Examples from Popular Fiction

It's a very popular trope in love stories when enemies or characters who antagonise one another learn to love one another. Although, it doesn't always make for the healthiest representations of romance.

For instance, Belle and the Beast start out as enemies when he kidnaps her father then locks her up, and through the course of the story they fall in love. In *You've Got Mail*, Tom Hanks runs a big bookshop chain that destroys Meg Ryan's character's career, and he manipulates her through email as he lies about who he is, until she falls in love with him.

In tales of friendship, it also works well, and is usually less riddled with problematic imagery. For instance, in *Trading Places* when Eddie Murphy and Dan Aykroyd are set against one another and through the story they become friends and work together to take down Duke & Duke. I did this in my first book—Lilly Prospero and Saffron Jones start out as enemies, then they learn to understand one another and become best friends.

Predictability

The downside of this trope, as with all tropes, is that it's predictable. Especially in a romantic comedy set up. There's no way you go into a film where the two lead characters are both attractive and charismatic and have wonderful chemistry, and you don't expect them to fall in love even whilst they're fighting at the beginning.

In *Calamity Jane*, Calam and Wild Bill sing a song early on about how much they dislike one another and by the end they're married. The passion is clear between them and everybody could see it coming.

However, as much as being predictable is a negative when you're writing stories as it can feel boring, and we always strive to be original and creative, there is something comforting and pleasurable about watching this trope play out. If everything else in your story is unpredictable and dramatic and your audience doesn't know what's coming, they can feel the tension and excitement from that, whilst knowing that at some point the two characters who hate each other right now are going to join up and either fall in love, or become friends or teammates who work together.

Why This Trope Can Work

When you see these characters separate, when they are obviously lacking something in their lives which you as the reader know is the other person, when they do finally come together it can feel triumphant. You know that now, with the effect they have on one another working in their favour, they can finally get what they want.

Whether it's cops who hate each other working together to take down the bad guy, or lovers who can finally find the happiness they've been craving, you know you're going to see the best these characters you've been bonding with have to offer.

If everything in your story is predictable, if it's trope after trope and nothing original happens, your audience will feel bored. However, with the clever use of one trope, such as this one, you can give them a positive feeling of being one step ahead and feeling excited to witness what they know is coming. It's like teasing them with a promise of something satisfying they know they want, and they know they'll get, whilst maintaining the rest of the story as something they have to experience fresh to know what will happen.

Keeping your audience intrigued or energised through the rest of the story makes sure that this trope doesn't get lost.

I do personally really enjoy this trope. As I say, the bond between Lilly and Saffron is something I particularly love. I enjoy writing their relationship because I find their dynamic is full of energy, and that is partly because they're somewhat mismatched and had to learn to care about one another rather than having immediate natural chemistry.

I think this trope can add a layer of conflict to a plotline which might otherwise feel a bit flat, and as long as you keep the rest of your story rich with new and exciting story, I really enjoy what this trope brings.

XXXVI
Death and Resurrection

The resurrection of characters that have died can be a dramatic game changer that enhances your story; however, if used too easily and without careful construction, it can have the opposite effect. Your audience can be left feeling like all the tension has been sapped away because if characters die it doesn't really mean anything. I'll be explaining why it can be a problem, also giving you techniques you can use to make it work for you.

Killing Your Characters

I've written previously about why killing main characters is a good way of ensuring your audience will feel the tension in scary or dramatic scenes, and you'll find that writers will embrace this by killing a favourite character in a big and dramatic way. It unseats the audience and makes them feel like the peril is real.

After you've killed them, you might be tempted to resurrect a character because it's a favourite that the audience likes to read or watch, and because the writer likes to write them, so they're brought back.

The Problem with Resurrection

The problem is, if characters are resurrected, you stop fearing their death. If you stop fearing their death, you fear everything less. The story is immediately less dramatic.

The other problem with resurrection is that it breaks the believability of the world. If you have a character who is able to resurrect people, why aren't they doing it all the time? Why aren't they saving people's lives and changing the world? Why this character, why now? And is that the only person in the world who can do that, is that the only person in history who can do that? Why aren't people being resurrected all over the place? But if they're the only person who can do it, does that power die with them? And again, it feels like a massive coincidence that the only person with that power happens to be right nearby your character when needed.

Having the potential for resurrection existing in the world of your story opens up an enormous mine of questions. You need to have a really carefully constructed reason for why this power exists where it does, and why it isn't used more liberally.

The Consequences of Resurrection

That said, resurrection can be written well. But it has to be done carefully, and with a real focus on the consequences.

If you're using a magic spell or potion to bring someone back, make sure that something used in that magic is incredibly rare and difficult to get, so it's a challenge and cannot be repeated. Making the resurrection of your character a one-time only thing maintains the tension as the potential for a final death is still very present. It also provides potential for conflict over whether it's morally acceptable to use this once in a lifetime resurrection potion on that person, and who, if anyone, is worthy.

In *Harry Potter and the Philosopher's Stone*, it's revealed that unicorn blood does not quite have resurrection potential, but the ability to keep someone alive if they're moments from death. However, the consequences are a big deal, as unicorns are perfectly pure and killing one to drink its blood is an incredibly dark and evil thing. You don't get to do it without a terrible downside, and good people would never make that decision because of those consequences, which is why Voldemort doing it was such a big deal.

It's important to make sure that the potential for resurrection exists prior to the actual resurrection happening. You don't want it to feel convenient or ill thought out. Foreshadow it carefully so that you build towards it and it feels significant.

Jon Snow in *Game of Thrones*

In *Game of Thrones*, they ended season five with Jon Snow being stabbed to death and left bleeding out in the snow. It was dramatic and powerful, and even though characters were regularly killed off in that show, Jon Snow had been a primary hero of the story from the start and killing him felt like a huge deal. However, very early in season six, he was resurrected by The Red Woman.

In theory this is fine. Her power to resurrect had been demonstrated before, it didn't come out of nowhere, but the impact was that the potential for Jon Snow's death didn't feel quite as final or important in future scenes, and the audience felt they'd been lied to. It felt like his death was leveraged as bait to bring the audience back for more, rather than being an actual part of the story, so the seeds of mistrust were sewn.

Lilly Prospero and the Magic Rabbit

I have written death and resurrection of a character. With as few spoilers as possible, in *Lilly Prospero and the Magic Rabbit*, a character dies and is brought back. The reason I feel it works is that it wasn't done for the drama of a death, and the convenience of wanting to keep writing a character.

The resurrection is a key moment in Lilly's power development, and it shapes her journey through not only that story, but beyond. The resurrection itself has a lasting impact on the character who comes back that carries into the subsequent stories and for the rest of their lives. And the reason it's not a repeated action that could be done any time is dealt with due to the consequences and the price that is paid.

How To Write Resurrection Well

My advice to anyone who wants to write a resurrection is to not make it a convenient small moment written so you get the drama of death but then get to keep writing the character. Treat it as the significant and enormous event it is. To bring someone back from the dead is a world changing event. It should be massive; it should have far reaching impact. It should have an effect on the person who did the resurrection, there is a massive moral question associated with it, and on the person that was resurrected because they experienced actual death. There would be long-term mental and emotional impact for that decision.

How to Write a Story

For the most part I think if you kill a character, they should stay dead. The only time you should see them again is in a different timeline; for instance, *Lost* allows us to revisit dead characters regularly in different timelines, but in the present day, death should be mostly final.

If you're going to resurrect someone, treat it as the enormous event it is, and don't exploit your audience by showing them a dead body and letting them feel the subsequent emotions, before washing them out later in a convenient little bit of magic so you can keep writing them consequence-free. Treat your audience and characters with respect by making the death and the resurrection matter.

XXXVII
How to Write Plot Twists

A plot twist is a sudden change in your story that your audience don't see coming, such as a reveal that one of the goodies is actually a baddie. Your plot twist can be written in a way that pulls your audience into your story and makes them want more because it's a really unexpected moment that's exciting to read, or it can boot them out. And you never want to boot your audience out.

The Wrong Way to Write a Plot Twist

If you want to throw a plot twist into your story, but without any thought or care, it's pretty easy. You just write until you get to a point where you feel a plot twist would energise your story, and then suddenly pull the rug out under your audience and change things. It comes out of nowhere and shocks your audience because they didn't see it coming.

The problem with this kind of plot twist is that your audience is unlikely to buy it, and it'll read like you as the writer didn't see it coming either.

If you have a character suddenly betray your Protagonist, or an unlikely hero suddenly get strength to be the one to fight the monster, but there has been no build up at all, no hint that it was coming, then it just feels like a random event that nobody will believe. A good plot twist has to be both believable, *and* a surprise. Just a surprise on its own isn't good enough.

Foreshadowing

The key to writing a plot twist that is still believable is in the foreshadowing. When your audience reads or watches your story for the second, third, fourth time, they should start to notice all the hints and clues throughout your story that the twist is coming.

Subtle signs baked into the story that, in and of themselves, are completely innocent moments that can go by unnoticed, which is why you don't see them on the first viewing, but when you add them all together, they're an arrow pointing to the arrival of the twist. Because even though you don't necessarily realise they're happening, because you're focusing on the main plot, you've still absorbed that information, so when the twist is revealed you might be surprised and excited by it, but you're not shocked out of the story because it actually does make sense.

Shazam!

An example I'm going to give you of a plot twist is the end of *Shazam!* so if you haven't seen it, go watch it. Because this is going to be full of spoilers.

In *Shazam!*, it seems like it'll be the "one superhero with the power" story that we know and love; Shazam is whizzing around the place and fighting the bad guy. However, at the end, he uses the wizard's staff (if you've never seen this film and are reading this anyway, I can't imagine how bizarre this whole thing sounds, but go with me) to put the powers of Shazam into his foster siblings. They then transform into a little team of six superheroes, ready to fight the monsters.

The reason it's such a great twist is because from the very beginning of the story it's trickled through events that this is coming. At the beginning the wizard talks about his brothers and sisters, that there were six of them, then in the foster home Billy refuses to accept five foster siblings as actual siblings until the end of the film. It's reinforced by the line of six chairs in the wizard's chambers, showing you that six people are supposed to have control of these powers. His foster brother, Freddy, is obsessed with superheroes and desperate to have the strength and ability to fight off bullies.

Because you're focused on the plot of Billy Batson searching for his birth mother, Shazam learning to use his powers, and Doctor Sivana's plot to use the Seven Deadly Sins, you don't really focus on those hints. There's no spotlight shone on them; they're just integrated into part of the story.

Other plot twist examples include *The Sixth Sense*, the fact he's been dead all along has been hinted at the whole way through. In *Harry Potter and the Philosopher's Stone*, Quirrell secretly being in league with Voldemort (and Voldemort secretly being *in* Quirrell) is hinted at from the first time you meet him.

Make the Hints Subtle

The key to writing a good plot twist is that the hints for the plot twist are not the focus of the story, but they happen all the way through, so when the twist happens it makes sense.

How to Write a Story

The way to avoid shining a light on your hints is to make sure there's another reason to show the information you're giving. It's integrated into another part of the story, so even though you're lining up your frogs for the big reveal at the end, in and of that moment, the frog is just part of an existing storyline. So in *Shazam!* when the wizard says "The seats of our brothers and sisters await!" it's lost in a sea of other strange speech patterns and information being delivered in a confusing and cryptic way, so even though he's specifically telling you that Billy's siblings will sit on those chairs, it's not focused on and gets blended into the rest of the scene.

To write a really solid plot twist, remember; all the hints you put through your story that the twist is coming shouldn't be distracting enough to make you aware that they're hints for what's to come, and they should be so integrated into your story that it makes sense they're included even if they're not building to a twist. Then, when they are all tied together by the plot twist at the end, it's incredibly satisfying. But a plot twist without any foreshadowing is just confusing and unbelievable.

XXXVIII
Writing Info Dumps

Sometimes as part of your story, you'll have information that needs to be delivered in order for the story to make sense. This could be rules of magical lore within your fictional universe, or information about a mission your character is going on.

You need either your audience, or both your character *and* your audience, to understand something important about your world for your story to make sense.

What is an "Info Dump?"

You can deliver this information in a way known as "info dumping". Sometimes this comes as one character lecturing another character about the history of the world that they're in, or the quest they have to go on. Alternatively, you write the narrator explaining everything the audience needs to know in paragraph after paragraph of information.

The aim is to ensure the audience absorbs the relevant information to understand the story and what's going on.

As You Know...

The crudest and most heavy-handed version of this is when one character says to another, "As you know..." and proceeds to explain the situation that the other character does indeed know, in order to tell the audience.

When you're the audience, this always sounds peculiar because there's no reason for the character to explain a situation in that way to another character who's familiar with the world. I wouldn't say to my partner before telling him something, "As you know, we have three children and a dog..." because he is aware of that so whatever I tell him subsequently would already make sense without that context being laid out for him.

A better version is the "Captain's Log" or diary, where the information is delivered in a way that tells the audience what's going on without an eyeroll as it's communicated to someone else, as the character is speaking to themselves. But it's still clunky.

The Problem with Info Dumps

When the narrator delivers the information, usually world building information about the history of worlds or wars, it can be incredibly tedious. It can often be found in a prologue.

Info dumping in this way can be very hard for the audience to comprehend or remember, it's heavy and detailed and, because it's pre-story and therefore you might not know any of the characters it's relevant to yet, lacking humanity.

The Lord of the Rings has a long info dump of world building describing the history of the rings and the lands that they went to. I realise that for many people that book (and those films) are treasured and beloved, but for a lot of other people it's just too heavy and too dry.

Why Info Dumps Happen

If you're building a big world or need your audience to understand something significant because it will become relevant later on in your story, I can understand the temptation to info dump.

You have put time and energy into constructing your world. You need some details to prop it up for the sake of the audience appreciating what it is you've done.

I write urban fantasy, so I don't need to construct the world my stories are told in. If you're telling high fantasy or deep space, you have to at least paint a canvas for your story to play out on, because people won't have an immediate picture in their head of your world.

Info Woven into The Story

If you look at *Star Wars: Episode IV – A New Hope* as an example, you don't go into that world with an immediate knowledge of the planets or the politics. George Lucas wanted to treat the first film like it was one in a series, so he treated the audience like they already knew everything they had to know. The text block at the beginning catches you up on the most recent events but doesn't info dump context for the entire story.

Despite this, you can watch those films and you catch up on everything you need to know during the course of the film. The details are woven into the story by what the characters do, and by Obi Wan teaching Luke. As Luke learns about the world and the magical destiny he is connected to, so does the audience.

An Entry Point Character

An entry point character is a way of depicting the world to the audience at the same time as it is depicted to the character. This avoids an "as you know" situation, because the character doesn't know; Luke doesn't know how to use The Force, he has to be taught, so he learns as the audience learns.

It also makes explaining the world they're in natural, because the outsider wants to learn and understand it and that then becomes part of the story. The children going through the wardrobe into Narnia in *The Lion, the Witch and the Wardrobe* learn with the audience. I previously wrote about taking your characters from the mundane to the magical, and this is part of why it's so effective.

Your Protagonist Isn't an Expert

The key is to deliver information to the audience that they need to know in a way that they want to know it, and that means you should give them a character who doesn't know everything, and has a story relevant reason to need to know it. Whether it's the politics or the history of the world, somebody needs to be enough of an outsider that they have reason to learn.

Your Protagonist is never the most powerful and knowledgeable wizard of the realm, because then they already know everything and there's no access point for your audience. You don't tell your story about the Jedi master who has already mastered use of The Force and has nothing to learn.

Fantasy World Characters Learning Info

You don't have to send an outsider from our world into your magical world to explain the world without info dumping. A character that has always lived in the world you're writing about can be your entry point character as long as they don't know what they need to know for the conflict you're telling.

You can demonstrate the basics of the world they're in by their interactions and activities prior to the inciting incident, and then the more complex details that your audience needs to learn can be new to your character too. That allows your character to learn at the pace your audience learns, and in a human way that they can relate to and be intrigued by, because it's part of your story and interesting to witness.

As long as there is information your Protagonist has to learn about the world you've created, your audience will want to learn about that world too, and you can deliver that information at a natural pace without the need to info dump.

Info Dumping is Boring

I tend to think that if you have to endure an info dump to get something from the story, then this is a badly told story. I don't go to my fiction to study, I am not looking to need to retain facts and figures, historical dates, or complex political details in my brain in order to enjoy a story. I go to my fiction to be entertained.

I can cope with a clunky info dump, like the "as you know" or "Captain's Log" method; I may be rolling my eyes but I won't leave a story over it, whereas as soon as a heavy duty info dump is piled onto me I am booted straight out. A bit of exposition you can get away with, but info dumping is boring, tedious and unnecessary.

XXXIX
Perfecting Your Prose to Dialogue Ratio

If your book is too dialogue heavy, it can read like a script. You don't get to know the environment your characters are in or connect with their interiority in a way that you can relate to their emotions. However, if your book is too prose heavy, it can make it hard to get to know the characters because so much of how we ground ourselves in our characters is in how they communicate with each other. So, it's important to strike a good prose to dialogue ratio.

Technically there is no right or wrong answer, you can't give an exact ratio number, because it's a matter of personal taste. For some people, the heavy layered prose, the lengthy descriptions and flowery language, is what appeals in fiction. So, if you love to write in that style, and your audience loves to read in that style, then there's no need to stop doing that. However, talking in general terms, for a broader and less niche appeal, finding a balance is important.

Make Your Story Easy to Read

When you drop too much prose, your readers can be left wondering who's spoken. I've had to count down lines from the last character marker to work out who said a pertinent line in a long conversation. Whilst you don't want to put "Jon said" and "Jude said" on every single line in a conversation, because in a conversation between two people that's going to be pretty obvious, if you drop the prose to the point where it's confusing, you're going to boot your audience out because they're putting effort into working out who spoke rather than thinking about what they're saying.

Who knows what, and how they deliver that information, is very plot relevant so it should be obvious to the reader when they do it. Confusion over who spoke is a writing failure.

As soon as you're outside of the story trying to work out who spoke, you're no longer absorbed by the story and the words on the page, you're outside that story trying to fight your way back in but blocked by the fact you need to do maths down the page to work out how to get back on track.

If you have a very conflict-dense scene where two characters are arguing passionately on either side of a moral dilemma, such as whether or not they should kill the bad guy, it could be obvious who spoke based on their opinions without needing character markers, so technically you could get away without it. But, it's important to remember, reading a script is a very different experience to reading a book.

Set the Scene

Even if your characters are clearly labelled, a script is a working document designed to be used to create a story where the actors, the director, the cinematographer, the set designers, are filling in the spaces around those lines. In a book, you have nobody to do that work for you. You need to provide that information to allow your audience to see in their head where your characters are and how they're feeling about it based on their actions and emotions. If your story is not alive with prose, it's not a relaxing read, because your audience has to try and fill in the spaces around the words themselves.

Dropping the dialogue so much that you never get to know your characters because you're spending so much time describing what they look like, the room they're in, the smell of the air, the emotions your characters feel, means your audience will get bored.

We want to read your characters communicating with one another, because your story is about what a character wants and how they go about getting it, and that means they have to communicate those wants. If they never go after something or want something, because you're too busy describing things around them, then your character will have no humanity. Humanity in a character is what draws your audience into caring enough about them to read their story to the end.

Keep Your Story Moving Forwards

Prose-heavy writing can lead to your story standing still. A stagnant story feels like a trudging read. Action, motivation and conflict keep the story dynamic and you need characters to communicate and disagree, and it keeps your story alive and interesting.

If you're going nowhere, moving towards nothing, because you're just describing everything instead of having your characters be busy, there's no draw for your reader to keep reading. As soon as your readers can't be bothered to read one book, they won't bother coming back to any future books, and you're going to lose your audience.

Using a Point of View Character

A good way to find a balance is to stick to a point of view character in your scene. Focus on how that one character feels about what's going on, the place they're in, how they feel about the other character's behaviour. If you stick to one character in that scene you can build your prose around them, but you're less likely to go on at length with rambling prose because your character is focused on the scene at hand, but you will give descriptions and details because your character will have emotions and feelings about the scene.

A point of view character doesn't know how everybody else feels, they know how *they* feel. They don't focus on every detail in the room they're in, but they do focus on what affects them directly. Your readers get to know the environment and feelings through their prose directly, but you still have the dialogue. Your characters will communicate with your point of view character and you'll get their interpretation of how those other characters behave, and you'll have your point of view character communicate with others and see what they choose to reveal and how they choose to reveal it.

With different point of view characters you have the opportunity to flex prose-heavy muscles if you do enjoy the flowery language, because different characters will have different personalities and different interiorities. If one of your characters has a description dense style, you can get that style into your story, but not so much that it's a constant tedious read. You just have to make sure they're balanced against less prose-heavy characters.

Find Your Own Style

As always, if you find an audience that particularly likes to read scripts, and you particularly like to write scripts, then you're fine. If you like to write lengthy descriptions and find an audience that likes to read them, then crack on. But mostly, a balance is important.

Your story can lean more towards prose, or more towards dialogue, but finding a way to get both the story and conflict being active through the dialogue, and enough description that your audience has an emotional connection to your characters, is what to aim for.

XL
How to Write Chapter One

A lot goes into writing a good story, and it takes a lot of chapters to complete one. But your first job is to write Chapter One, and that is where a lot of people freeze. Not because you don't know what to do with the rest of your story, but because you don't know how to start it.

I'll be talking through things you need to include to write Chapter One of your book, and hopefully leaving you feeling empowered to make that step. The world needs more stories, let's make yours one of them.

Who Is Your Protagonist?

Your Protagonist is your main character. That's the person whose shoulders you will be riding on for the majority of the story. So, you probably have the clearest idea of who this person is in your head.

Your story is following your Protagonist on their journey to try and get what they want. So, to make that make sense, you need to demonstrate what is missing in their lives. As you introduce your main character, let your readers discover what in their lives is frustrating them. Something is wrong enough that they are then motivated to change it.

How To Introduce Your Protagonist

To introduce them, don't start with them waking up in bed unless you absolutely have to. It's been done so many times, it's boring, and it tells you very little about who they are.

Start with them in their lives, living normally. Introduce them in their natural environment so you can tell the audience what about that environment is unsatisfactory.

You can introduce any side characters, show what they mean to your Protagonist by how they interact with one another. Going straight in with who your Protagonist is and the life they're living makes them feel real. That will help your audience understand who they're going to be following.

Who Is Your Antagonist?

Your Antagonist is probably the "bad guy" of your story. It actually means the opponent set against the Protagonist, so they're not necessarily a bad person. The point of the Antagonist is that what they want is in direct conflict with what the Protagonist wants.

Whatever it is your Protagonist wants, your Antagonist wants to stop them having it. This could be because your Antagonist wants the exact same thing and they can't both have it. Or your Protagonist wants something that will block your Antagonist from getting what they want.

For instance, imagine your Protagonist is a teenager who wants to go to the Prom with the captain of the football team. In this story, your Antagonist will *also* want to go to the Prom with the same person. They can't both have what they want, someone has to lose.

Alternatively, your Protagonist is a teenager who just wants to go to the Prom. In this case, your Antagonist wants to stop them for their own reasons. They could be an overprotective parent who wants them to stay home, or a teacher who wants to put them in a detention. But your Protagonist can't both *go* and *not go*. Someone has to lose.

How To Introduce Your Antagonist

In the scope of your story, your Antagonist is as important as your Protagonist. You need your Protagonist to tell your story about, and you need your Antagonist to make it entertaining.

You can introduce your Antagonist first, show what they want. This works well if they're actually a bad person, because then when you meet your Protagonist it's a relief. It's likely that what the bad person wants is what motivates your Protagonist, because they need stopping.

For instance, in *Lilly Prospero and the Mermaid's Curse*, first I introduced The Harvester. He is dragging a mermaid from the ocean, ready to carve her up and sell her body parts on the magical black market. You know what he wants, because he's doing it. Then, when you cut to Lilly and Saffron, you know that they will become motivated to stop him and that's the story you'll be following.

Alternatively, introduce your Protagonist first, then when you show what's frustrating about their lives, you can incorporate the Antagonist into it. For instance, when you first meet Harry Potter his life is unsatisfactory. He's living in the cupboard under the stairs, and he has a miserable existence. There are multiple Antagonists but looking at the Dursleys and Voldemort, without Voldemort, he wouldn't be there in the first place.

Without the Dursleys treating him so terribly, his life would be happier. Harry wanting to change his life is directly related to the way his Antagonists have impacted his life.

What is the Inciting Incident?

You have no real story until your Protagonist and your Antagonist are set against one another. Your Protagonist is just living, and not actively in pursuit of anything. The Inciting Incident is what puts your story into motion. It establishes the conflict.

Without conflict your story is boring. Your Protagonist could just go and get what they want without any challenge or struggle. There's no point following that. Without conflict your scenes will be slow, and your story will be dull. The Inciting Incident is when you establish the story conflict and your audience connects with what will entertain them in this story.

Your Inciting Incident is when your Protagonist moves from passive to active. Either they realise what they want and go after it, or they realise what the Antagonist is doing and want to stop them. But that moment, something sparks them into action, and you need to show it happen.

Where Does the Inciting Incident Go?

The beginning of Chapter One can be them living their lives in passive mode. You use that to tell your audience who they are, who the people in their lives are, and demonstrate what they're frustrated by before they become motivated to change it.

However, you don't want to leave them passive for too long because then you're just delaying the start of your story. Your story is why your readers are there. Somebody just living isn't interesting, it's not a story, you need to set them in motion.

There's no limit to how early you put your Inciting Incident, because you can get to know who they are whilst they're active. However, my personal taste would be to spend a little time with them first. So, ideally, your Inciting Incident should come towards the end of Chapter One. You should spend a little time getting to know them and the Antagonist, so you understand why their motivation matters. Then, when you're established, set them at odds and your story is moving.

World Building

The world your story is set in needs to be clear to your readers in Chapter One. If it's in our world, tell your readers specifically where your character is. What country is your story set in, what work, or home environment are they in, and are any laws or rules going to impact them?

If your story is an urban fantasy, make sure it's clear that there is the potential for magic in that world. If you leave it too late it will feel like your genre changes suddenly. If your readers don't realise they're reading a book with magic, they could be booted out when it's introduced. Make it clear from Chapter One.

The world building in a High Fantasy Story will likely take longer than for any others. Whether your story is set in space or some fantasy world, there is a rich history and lore that needs exploring. For Chapter One, don't overwhelm with world building because it will feel tedious, and establishing characters is more important.

Chapter One needs to tell your readers what kind of world they're in, and it needs to focus on how it affects your Protagonist and Antagonist. You can build the world around them by how they move through it. Your audience can get a handle on what sort of environment it is by your character's homes, work, transport, and social lives. The history and lore should be dripped in through those interactions, rather than info dumped into Chapter One.

Setting Up Your Story

The purpose of Chapter One is to hook your reader, draw them into reading on, and to set up the rest of your story.

Make sure that by the end of Chapter One, your audience knows:

1) Who the Protagonist is and what they want - it tells your audience what story they'll be following and why they're bothering to read it.
2) Who the Antagonist is and what they want - it tells your audience why the Protagonist's journey matters and what the conflict of the story will be.
3) Where the story is taking place - without any understanding of the characters' environment, it'll feel like they're in a plain white box. You need to set the stage so they're humans not puppets.

If you establish those points in Chapter One, your audience will understand why they're there and what they're supposed to care about.

Be Brave

It's incredibly normal to find staring at a blank page intimidating. Starting Chapter One means you're actually taking the step to write this story you've been dreaming of writing. If you're actually writing it, you could actually fail. Until you try, you've got no risk.

But do it. Try it. Write it. The world needs stories, and your voice matters. Nobody in the world can tell your story like you can, and that's a special and unique power to wield. Your thoughts, your life, your history and beliefs all matter, and stories are how you can communicate those things to the world.

If you write Chapter One, you're then on your way. You're a writer. Until you've written you're just an aspiring writer, so make that transition.

When you get to the end of your story, you'll probably want to change some things about Chapter One and that's absolutely fine. We all do that. Editing is a normal and essential part of writing. It doesn't have to be perfect; it just has to be written. Until it's written you can't edit it and make it perfect.

XLI
How to Track Your Continuity

Your story "continuity" is making sure that, from one scene to another, nothing changes about the people or the environment they're in that wasn't intended to change and was controlled by the writer.

In film and TV, continuity errors can happen due to wardrobes changing suddenly, placement of props on the set, or weather, but I'll be focusing specifically on the written word because as a writer the story continuity is your responsibility to control.

What is a Continuity Error?

Continuity errors can occur when the writer forgets a small detail about the characters, such as eye colour, when you forget what backstory you've previously revealed, such as family or past relationships, or when you fail to track your character's emotional state from one scene to the next.

When you forget a detail, it's usually something so small that it slips past you unnoticed because of how much you're already remembering. Because your audience isn't burdened with the task of remembering everywhere the characters have been, and everywhere they're going, they're more likely to notice the mistakes.

What Do Continuity Errors Do?

When your audience notices a continuity error it boots them out of the story. Readers are left wondering if the mistake was intentional and if it was, then why write it, or they're wondering what the truth of that character is. Which part of the story was the error? When your audience is outside the story looking in, trying to work out what they're meant to be thinking, you've lost their attention and you've lost their trust.

You need your audience to put themselves in your hands completely and rely on you to get them to the story climax uninterrupted. If your audience feels you're a careless or unreliable storyteller, they are never going to fully invest in your story, even if they're curious about the climax, they won't completely connect to it.

Why Do Continuity Errors Happen?

The first thing to remember is that continuity errors, in first drafts especially, are common and not a problem. You're trying to create an entire world and manage and construct the lives of multiple people within it.

If this your second, third, fourth book in a series, you're not only managing the lives as they currently are, but you're trying to keep the lives and events of all their former stories in your head too. If you've written things outside of that series, you're trying to keep your head on which characters you're writing now, and not letting the history blur into your other works.

My first book, *Lilly Prospero and the Magic Rabbit*, came out in 2016. Since then I've written two other adult books, a children's book, a TV show and a film. That is a lot of life, a lot of history and events that I'm trying to manage in my own head as well as vaguely keeping track of my own existence. Normal people, the non-story tellers, only have to keep on top of their own life. I couldn't possibly tell you every tiny detail of every event in my first book, Lilly Prospero And The Magic Rabbit, but I'm currently working on the third instalment in that series.

How To Track Your Continuity

The first thing to do is to edit thoroughly. A first draft is allowed to be messy, that's what it's for. But then your job is to fix it. Read it, fix it, read it again and fix it again. Then send it to your proof-reader, who will read it and notice the details you've missed.

Editing is an essential part of a writer's job, and it can turn your scruffy mess of an idea blob into a beautifully crafted story that will draw your audience in and emotionally connect with them.

I highly recommend recording details about your characters that you can refer back to, especially if you've written multiple stories. I have spreadsheets detailing everything about each character in every story.

I include family, friendships, enemies, magical powers, eye colour, hair colour, personality traits, etc, and any key events that have impacted them and in what story that event occurred. My writing and editing process is hugely aided by knowing I can check my character details and make sure that what I'm writing is consistent with my previous work.

In terms of scene-level continuity, rather than over arcing details such as appearance or history, be dedicated to tracking how each character feels and making sure they behave accordingly. If you've shown a character to be angry in a previous scene, you need to tell your audience they've either moved on from it, by showing it in your story, or maintain that emotion. If it's simply slipped away and your audience wasn't shown when or why, that character has been broken. Consistent emotions are a real key to making your characters feel real; broken character continuity breaks the story.

Keeping track of your continuity gets harder the more you write, but it's also more important the more you write. Put real effort into it, record your characters in whatever way makes most sense to you, and you'll find your story is better because of it.

XLII
Editing

Editing is a really important part of your writing, and it's something that all writers have to learn to do well if they want to be successful. However, it also has a bit of a bad rep. Editing hell. Hopefully I'll be able to both teach you how to edit your book or script well, and also how to enjoy the process.

Turning Your First Draft into Something Beautiful

When I talk about editing, I'm not talking about using your spell check. I'm talking about how to take a first draft and turn it into something that reads like it was carefully designed and composed from the beginning, with all the loose ends tied up, and the climax built towards like a strategic plan.

The editing process is how to make your book or script feel completely satisfying and enjoyable for your audience, rather than just a story they're experiencing and then moving on from without a second thought. It's how to take a perfectly fine story and make it excellent.

Don't Be Scared of Making Mistakes

The first thing to remember is you cannot edit a blank page. If you're so worried about making your story brilliant that you never even start it, you will never accomplish even an adequate story. Instead of being too scared to start, embrace the fact that first drafts can be messy and make no sense, and that getting to the end of it is all you need to do.

The editing process is where you can take that messy first draft and make it something to be proud of, and nobody has to see that first draft except you. The purpose of the first draft is to just get the story out.

First Drafts

The first draft is a lot of discovery because unless you plot every moment in advance, which I don't, you'll learn a lot about your story as you go. And that can leave loose ends that need tidying up.

When you first start writing, you might not be certain of where your story is going so it can be meandering. You might know the beginning and end but not be sure of how your characters are getting there. During the writing of your story, you might add or remove characters depending on what it turns out you need. Editing is how you smooth it all out, and make it seem like you always knew what you were doing.

When you edit, you take that first draft and weave in the clever details that make your story work so well. Editing is where you can add narrative triplets, weave in set up and pay off, and craft clever foreshadowing. All these details that are nearly impossible to write them from the start, but nobody needs to know they weren't. That's the magic.

My Editing Process

I'll use an example from the book I'm working on. I'm writing a book about a character named Ivy Rhodes. She's a woman who has gone through a marital breakdown and has to go on a path of self-discovery to learn who she is and what she wants in life independently.

I felt like the story was fine but when I got to the end, I felt like I needed something after the climax to show her settled in her new life. I wanted something symbolic as an end note to finally tie a bow on the story, so it didn't just fade out without any meaning.

To do this I utilised a narrative triplet. I created a matchstick house for her, something she had made in her childhood and that her ex-husband never liked, but that she was very proud of. I went back into the earlier parts of the story to weave it in and build to the end of the book more neatly.

In her marriage, she'd kept the matchstick house in a cupboard out of sight. In the middle of the book she was able to have it out but didn't feel it had a place to live. At the end of the book, as a final acknowledgement of the journey she has been on, the matchstick house has a place to live, on display.

It works as a demonstration of how she has come to accept who she is, and be proud of who she is, and is in a situation in which who she is celebrated not ignored. It's a simple detail, but representative of Ivy's journey in a way that feels composed from the beginning, even though it wasn't. Being able to go back and edit that detail improved the story, and the connection to Ivy as a person.

Edit Your Protagonist's Story Arc

When you get to the end of your story, you will be able to look at your story with a richer understanding of your protagonist and their journey.

Think of something to layer into the earlier stages of the story to show their journey, much like Ivy's matchstick house, then you go back into your story. Mention it in one context in the first act, again in the second act in a slight development from the first, and then in the third act, at the end of your story, you subvert that so it's now demonstrating their state at the end, in a narrative triplet.

Learning who your character is, and getting to know them well, is the key to doing this. The matchstick house is showing an open wound in the first mention, it's poking it in the second, and it's healing it in the third.

Editing in Foreshadowing

To make the climax of your story more satisfying, again you need to go back into the earlier part of your story and edit in the foreshadowing for it. Expert level foreshadowing, that really elevates the quality of your story, requires that anything at the end of the story appears earlier in the story.

If your character uses a weapon or tool in a fight, mention that weapon or tool in a different context in the beginning of the story. If they use a piece of information, show them learning it for a different reason. If they have to go to a certain place, have them visit that place earlier. Anything that is plot relevant at the end of the story needs to be plot relevant for a different reason at the beginning.

Any appearances in the earlier part of your story need to work in and of themselves as part of the plot, rather than standing out as having been crowbarred in, and therefore a light is shone on it.

Subtlety is better, and more satisfying for those who have noticed it and remembered it.

If you get to the end of your story, you can create the illusion of foreshadowing by plucking details from the beginning and using them at the end. A magic spell, a weapon, a hobby or skill. Anything can be utilised at the end that you mentioned simply as world building or character development in the beginning. It creates the same effect as weaving a later detail in earlier, you're just doing it in reverse.

Editing Your Continuity

After you've taken the time to stitch in the clever writing techniques, it's time to focus on continuity. Read your story, read it again. Note any significant events and make sure they're always relevant, track your characters' emotional states, check how things are described and make sure it's consistent.

If the last time you wrote a character they were in the clutches of despair or heartache, you need to carry that into their next scene. Even if they've moved on and are not still in the same pain, acknowledge that they were previously, or it'll look like a forgotten detail. If you've described one place as a certain distance from another, make sure that's represented in travel time descriptions.

It's very easy to forget tiny details when you're carrying and constructing an entire world in your head, but your audience will not forget. If you don't bother to check your continuity and keep it neat, you'll boot them out of the story and lose their attention. You need to make sure your audience feels like they're in the stable hands of a storyteller who knows their work inside out.

Proofreading

When you've got your book to the best version of it you can, it's time to send it for proofreading. Find a proofreader you trust, someone who notices the tiny details, someone who appreciates the effort that goes into the foreshadowing and narrative triplets so that when it hasn't quite worked, they can explain why.

Find someone who is honest, not your mum or your partner who might feel they need to flatter you. Find a professional. I use Steph Warren of "Bookshine and Readbows" and can highly recommend her services.

Editing Matters

Ultimately, you need to remember that taking the time to edit your book is as important as taking the time to write it in the first place. When you start to appreciate the joy of breathing life and craft into the bones of a story, you will start to enjoy the process of editing.

It's exciting to find ways to weave the beginning into the end, plucking insignificant moments from the beginning of the story and making them important at the end, and crafting narrative triplets that make every important moment feel special.

Your story will be elevated because you've put in the time, and you, as a writer, will be giving your craft the time and love it deserves.

XLIII
Writer's Block

Writer's block is a common problem that many writers struggle with. It is where you cannot move forward with your story and any menial task, such as laundry or vacuuming, suddenly becomes much more appealing to you than actually putting words on the page because of how hard you're finding it to write.

I'll be talking you through common causes of writer's block, and things you can do to move through it and find your way back into your story.

Your Scene Lacks Conflict

I find that writer's block is more likely strike me when there's a reason my story isn't moving forwards. The way your story will naturally move forward is with active conflict. If the scene or section of your story that you're working on has an active and busy conflict, you'll have plenty to write about and it won't feel stuck.

If I've written myself into a situation where it's stalled, there's no conflict, there's nothing obvious to write about. If the protagonist is not actively in pursuit of their goal, then I get lost and I can't write anymore.

You might find that you're writing events happening, people are talking, there are things going on, but it's not actually story essential. Even if it's momentarily entertaining, you know inside that you're not contributing to your story in a real way. It feels like trudging through sand when you read it back. It is slow and meaningless.

As stunted as your story feels, it makes your emotional connection to your story even more stunted, and then you're blocked from accessing it again.

What Does Your Character Want?

To deal with this kind of writer's block, you need to refocus your energy on what your character wants, how they're going about getting it, and what's stopping them from having it. Reconnect with how your character is feeling emotionally about their situation and the people around them.

Go back into your story to the last point they were actively in pursuit of their goal. Delete everything after that point and start again, with that in mind. It might be a lot of work, but if it's work you're not connected to it's worth ditching.

Understanding why you're telling this part of your character's life is key. If you're telling a meaningless story, just a snapshot out of their life where they're not in pursuit of anything and there's no conflict, it'll quickly feel dull and you'll feel blocked.

Ask yourself why now? Why this story, why this person, why this moment in their life? Focus on that, find that, and you'll find you way back into your story.

Your Scenes Are Flat

Another kind of writer's block you might experience is if everything in the scene is moving forward as it needs to, information is coming out, everyone is focused and the conflict is active, but the scene feels flat.

When you read over what you've written you're aware it does what it needs to do but it doesn't excite you. It will drain your connection, leave you feeling like your story is dull. Even if everything else you've done up to that point is exciting and works well, that scene can lose you, block you.

Add an Additional Layer of Activity

In this situation, you need to give your scene some flavour. If your characters are talking about something and reacting to it, go into that scene and give one of the characters a secondary task. They're not just discussing the issue that moves your plot along, they're busy with something else that almost interrupts the flow.

By adding a secondary task, you're adding a layer of conflict. It could be a secondary conversation point about a thing they're excited to do and want to steer the conversation to, or it could be a literal task such as cooking or a craft that is important to them. When the information the scene needs to deliver comes out with more of a challenge and extra layers of interest, it makes the scene feel more exciting and dynamic and holds the attention more.

If you feel entertained by the story you're writing, you will free yourself from the block. Entertainment is the whole point.

Insecurity

It is important to remember that loathing of your own work is normal. We're creatives, and creatives are often very emotional, and prone to self-loathing and self-doubt. But your brain is lying to you. Hating your work in the moment does not mean you will always hate your work.

When your writer's block is caused by that insecurity and panic about your own ability, you have to try and fight it. Because you are the only person who can tell your story in the way you tell it, and your voice matters.

This is one of my main causes of writer's block. I am chronically insecure about my work, and often struggle to move through it. But, if you love the job as I do, you owe it to yourself to try.

First Drafts Are Messy

First drafts are often messy and full of problems, and that's okay. If your writer's block is caused by awareness that your work isn't perfect, you need to remember that editing is how you fix that. It's not the job of the first draft to be a perfect story, it's the job of the first draft to just exist.

Editing is how you shape what you've written into something beautiful and pleasing to read. You can add the extra dimensions of entertainment into flat scenes, cull scenes that don't move the story along, and weave in clever and interesting writing techniques such as narrative triplets that make your story feel professional and composed with skill.

Write through the feeling that your work sucks. Push through it. If your Protagonist has fallen off the path of pursuing their goals, steer them back in that direction. If your scenes feel flat, you might need to add some flourishes, but the scene can still work in and of itself. Write through it if you can.

Feeling Creatively Empty

If you can't write through it, you might just need a break. And that's okay. You might be empty creatively.

When we start writing and creating, we've been filled up with the work of others, inspired by books we've read and films we've watched, and we have so much to pour out that it feels easy. But we need to keep that supply filled, and if you feel drained then take some time out to go and read, or watch, and allow your creativity to be refilled.

Rest and allow yourself to be inspired by others. We aren't machines.

Read More
Siren Stories: The Ultimate Bibliography

Lilly Prospero And The Magic Rabbit (The Lilly Prospero Series Book 1)
By J.J. Barnes

Lilly Prospero And The Magic Rabbit is a young adult urban fantasy exploring the corrupting effects of absolute power on a teenage girl. When the unpopular and lonely Lilly Prospero is given a talking pet rabbit, her life begins to change. She is thrust into a world of magic, mystery, and danger, and has to get control of a power she doesn't understand fast to make the difference between life and death. The first in a new series by J.J. Barnes, Lilly Prospero And The Magic Rabbit is a tale full of excitement, sorrow and mystery, as Lilly Prospero shows just how strong a girl can be.
Available in Paperback and for Kindle.

Alana: A Ghost Story
By Jonathan McKinney

Alana is a ghost, trapped in the New York Film Academy dorms, where she died. She has friends, fellow ghosts, with whom she haunts the students living there, and passes her time watching whatever TV shows and movies the students watch.

But she is restless. She wants to move on. And when a medium moves into the dorms, Alana gets a nasty shock, which turns her mundane afterlife upside down.

Alana is a light yet moving short story about a miraculous love that travels many years and many miles to save a lost, trapped and hopeless soul.

Available in Paperback and for Kindle.

Emily the Master Enchantress: The First Schildmaids Novel (The Schildmaids Saga Book 1)
By Jonathan McKinney

Hidden, veiled behind the compressed wealth of New York City, is a dank underbelly of exploitation and slavery, which most people never see, or sense, or suffer. A cruel, expanding world.

And when Emily Hayes-Brennan, a proficient enchantress with a good heart and a tendency to overshare, is recruited to the world renowned crime fighters, the Schildmaids, she will find that that cruel world threatens to expand around her, and everyone she cares about.

She will be confronted by conflicts of fate and choice, as she seeks to find her place in the world.

Available in Paperback and for Kindle.

After the Mad Dog in the Fog: An Erotic Schildmaids Novelette
By Jonathan McKinney and J.J. Barnes

Emily Hayes-Brennan wants to get through a simple night out in her home city of New York, introducing her new boyfriend Teo to her friends, so she can get him home and have sex with him for the very first time. But when an obnoxious admirer and old flame shows up, she begins to fear that her plans are going awry.

After the Mad Dog in the Fog is a wild and energetic novelette about love and desire, and about the free joy that comes from prioritising the one you love before all others.

Available in Paperback and for Kindle.

Lilly Prospero And The Mermaid's Curse (The Lilly Prospero Series Book 2)
By J.J. Barnes

Lilly Prospero And The Mermaid's Curse is a young adult, urban fantasy following Lilly Prospero and her friend Saffron Jones on a magical adventure to Whitstable.

Whilst on a family holiday, Lilly and Saffron meet mermaids under attack from a mysterious and violent stranger, work with a powerful coven of witches, and fight to save not only the lives of the mermaids, but their own lives as well.

Available in Paperback and for Kindle.

The Inadequacy of Alice Anders: A Schildmaids Short Story
By Jonathan McKinney

Alice Anders can summon vision of the future, which guides her heroic friends through heroic acts. Sometimes she'll see vulnerable people in danger; sometimes she'll see her superhero friends in places where they can help those who can't help themselves.

But, for the last three and a half weeks, she's not been able to summon a single vision—and given that she started working for the superhero team of her dreams, the Schildmaids, exactly three and a half weeks ago, she's becoming anxious about her worth. And to figure out why her power has gone away, she'll have to push herself, and face some hard truths.

The Inadequacy of Alice Anders is a light and bittersweet short story about the pain of loss, and about facing that pain when it threatens to hold you down and hold you back.

Available in Paperback and for Kindle.

The Fundamental Miri Mnene: The Second Schildmaids Novel (The Schildmaids Saga Book 2)
By Jonathan McKinney

Miri Mnene is the Syncerus, a warrior, and the strongest of the Schildmaids, the New York team of legendary crime fighters. But she was not always the Syncerus. Once, she was the Xuétú Nánrén Shashou, the final student of the man-hating, man-killing Guan-yin Cheh.

And when she is sent to South Dakota to investigate a mystical brothel, which has been kidnapping women, kidnapping girls, and forcing them to work, she is confronted by the darkness that lives within her when her past and present collide.

The Fundamental Miri Mnene is a powerful novel about the lengths to which you should go, the lengths to which you must go, in order to see justice in the world.

Available in Paperback and for Kindle.

The Relief of Aurelia Kite: A Schildmaids Novella
By Jonathan McKinney

It is Christmas and Aurelia Kite is a young New Yorker, trapped in an abusive relationship, dreaming of escape. When her controlling boyfriend Trafford takes on a new job, her path crosses with two highly serious female crime fighters, causing her to make a big decision about what she will and will not tolerate.

The Relief of Aurelia Kite is a harsh novella with a soft centre, about hope in the face of toxic romance, and about the salvation that can be found just by talking to a sympathetic stranger.

Available in Paperback and for Kindle.

Not Even Stars: The Third Schildmaids Novel
By Jonathan McKinney

Teo Roqué is journeying through Europe with Emily Hayes-Brennan, the woman he loves, when ancient hostilities give way to a war between powerful, clandestine organisations. A war which puts the young couple's lives in danger, as well as all those they care about.

As a new threat emerges, fanning the conflict's flames, Teo and Emily must work together to end the war before it leads to a disaster much, much worse than they'd imagined.

Not Even Stars is an incredibly intense novel about all-consuming love, about awe-inspiring heroism, and about the cost of making the right choice when the fate of the world hangs in the balance.

Available in Paperback and for Kindle.

The Mystery of Ms. Riley: a Schildmaids Novella
By Jonathan McKinney

Alice Anders and Rakesha McKenzie are members of the Schildmaids, the legendary New York crime fighters. And when Alice sees visions of Nina Riley, a young New Yorker carrying a deep, hidden pain the two heroes fight to determine what has caused that pain, and how to save Ms. Riley from a prison she cannot even see.

The Mystery of Ms. Riley is a harsh yet hopeful story about self-doubt, about ordinary, everyday oppression, and about the kind of love that defies the testimonies of everyone around you.

Available in Paperback and for Kindle.

Unholy Water: A Halloween Novel
By Jonathan McKinney

In the misty Lancashire town of Ecclesburn, kids go missing. But no one talks about it. Everyone knows why, but they don't talk about it. The grown ups smear garlic and holy water over their necks and wrists while walking the dog after dark, but they never say the V word.

And when one of the local pubs is taken over by a group of undead monsters, and a trio of vampire hunters is called to clear them out, a terrible series of events begins to play out, which will change the way Ecclesburnians live forever.

Unholy Water is a dark and bloodthirsty novel about desire in wild excess, about whether you should defy your circumstances or adapt to them, and about the kind of inflexible determination that can save or destroy those that matter most.

Available in Paperback and for Kindle.

Emerald Wren and the Coven of Seven
By J.J. Barnes

As a child, Emerald's grandfather gives her a magic lamp with the promise that she can change the world. As an adult Emerald is working hard as a waitress by day, and as part of a crime fighting coven by night.

And when they get news of a man working his way across the country, burning women to death in his wake, Emerald's coven of seven must take on the biggest challenge of their lives, and risk everything to save the people they love.

Available in Paperback and for Kindle.

Nature-Girl Vs Worst Nightmare
By Rose McKinney and J.J. Barnes

Nature-Girl vs Worst Nightmare is the debut novel from then six-year-old Rose McKinney, with just a smidge of help from her mother, author J.J. Barnes.

Deep in the Sparkling Forest, Nature-Girl and her friends are training to be superheroes at Miss Sparkle's Academy for Magical Children.

When old enemy Worst Nightmare sends an army of Bad Dreams to attack the school, Nature-Girl must use everything she's learned, and face her biggest fears, if she's going to stop him.

Nature-Girl vs Worst Nightmare is the first book from the new Siren Smalls brand for Siren Stories, a collection of books for children aged 6-12, full of magic, adventure and danger.

Check out more at www.sirenstories.co.uk

Printed in Great Britain
by Amazon